FARSI

Farsi–English
English–Farsi

Dictionary
& Phrasebook

Nicholas Awde
&
Camilla Shahribaf

D0249835

HIPPOCRENE BOOKS INC
New York

Typeset & designed by Desert♥Hearts

For information, address:
HIPPOCRENE BOOKS, INC.
171 Madison Ave.
New York, NY 10016
www.hippocrenebooks.com

Library of Congress Cataloguing-in-Publication Data

Awde, Nicholas.
    Farsi : Farsi-English English-Farsi dictionary &
    phrasebook / Nicholas Awde & Camilla Shahribaf.
        p. cm.
    In English and Persian (roman).
    ISBN-13: 978-0-7818-1073-9
    ISBN-10: 0-7818-1073-6
        1. Persian language--Conversation and phrase
books--
    English. 2. Persian language--Dictionaries--English.
    3. English language--Dictionaries--Persian. I.
Shahribaf,
    Camilla. II. Title.

PK6239.A93 2006
491'.5583421--dc22

2006049666

CONTENTS

- An Iranian person is an **Irâni**.
- The adjective for Iranian is **Irâni**.
- Iranians call themselves **Irâniyân**.
- Iran is **Irân**.
- The Farsi, or Persian, language is **Fârsi**.

INTRODUCTION

Farsi, also known as Persian (**Fârsi**), is the mother tongue to more than 35 million speakers in Iran — about 50 percent of the population. There are several million more native speakers in neighboring Afghanistan and Pakistan (where it is called Dari), and Tajikistan (where it is known as Tajik). These three forms of Farsi are more or less mutually intelligible. While the distinction between Farsi and Dari Persian is analogous to the distinction between European French and Canadian French, Tajik, however, has become more distinct, largely as a result of Russian and western cultural and political constraints introduced when Tajikistan became one of the republics of the Soviet Union in the early part of the 20th century.

In Iran, Farsi is the country's official language and is used by the whole population as the language of government, the media, and school instruction. Of the rest of Iran's population, 25 percent speak related languages such as Kurdish, Luri, and Baluchi, while the remainder speak Arabic, Modern Aramaic (Assyrian), Armenian, Georgian, Romany, and Turkic languages such as Azerbaijani (there are 18-20 million speakers in Iran).

Historically, Persian was a more widely understood language in an area ranging from the Middle East to India. There are large populations of speakers in other Persian Gulf countries, especially Iraq, as well as Bahrain, Oman, Yemen, and the United Arab Emirates). There are also thriving communities in Europe and the USA, especially California.

Farsi is an Indo-European language, the same family that includes English, Spanish, Russian, and Hindi. It belongs to the West Iranian group that includes the closely related languages of Luri, and Bakhtiari. Other more distant relations include Kurdish, spoken in Iran, Iraq, and Turkey; Baluchi, spoken in Iran, Afghanistan, and Pakistan; and Pashto, spoken in Afghanistan and Pakistan.

Not spoken but still used today is Pahlavi (Middle Persian) — this is the language of the Avesta, the holy scriptures of the Zoroastrian religion (the nation's religion, founded by the prophet Zoroaster or Zarathustra, before the coming of Islam), and of other texts written since the 6th century B.C. The words Pahlavi, Persia and Farsi are derived from the Parthians, the warlike people who ruled Persia (known then as Pârsa or Fârs) after the collapse of Alexander's empire.

We also know Old Persian from the beautiful and detailed cuneiform inscriptions left by the mighty Achaemenid dynasty (559-331 B.C.) that ruled the Empire of the Aryans (from which name the word Iran is derived) until the conquests of the Macedonian emperor-king Alexander the Great.

Since the times of the first Arab conquests, Farsi has been written in a variety of the Arabic script called Perso-Arabic. Until recent centuries, it was easily the most prominent language after Arabic in the Middle East and regions beyond. For example, it was a lingua franca for commerce throughout Central Asia and the Indian Ocean. To the east, it became an important language during the reign of the Moguls in Indian where knowledge of Persian was cultivated and encouraged. To the west, a fusion of Turkish and Persian (which are unrelated linguistically) became the aspirational language of the sprawling Ottoman empire. In both Turkish and Indian courts Persian became the written language of scholars and scientists during the 15th to 18th centuries, and it was the language used by some of the world's most influential poets from this period. Indeed, it has been said that in the garden of Eden Adam and Eve spoke the soft cadences of Persian (the Archangels spoke the more strident Turkish).

Ancient nation

Better known today as the Islamic Republic of Iran (**Jomhuri-ye Eslâmi-ye Irân**), Iran is in fact one of the world's oldest continuous nations. Over the centuries, the commitment of its people to their independence has been an extraordinary story, adapting over the ages and absorbing foreign cultures and invaders with ease. Today an oil-rich Islamic republic, Iran has also been the Zoroastrian Empire of Classical Times, the Shi'ite bastion of the Islamic Empire, the dazzling Safavid realm of the 17th century.

But Iran has been also been invaded frequently and has seen its borders changed over the centuries. Invaded by Seljuk Turks, Mongols, and so many others — and often caught up in the affairs and wars of larger powers — Iran has always reasserted its national identity and has always reinvented itself, phoenix-like, as a distinct political and cultural entity. Invariably envied and coveted by its neighbors, the nation not only has been a constantly political force in the region but also a cultural one. The world's greatest creative forces include Omar Khayyam, Firdowsi, and Rumi whose *Masnavi* consists of six books containing 30,000 couplets, considered to be the most profound and brilliant work of Farsi literature, the sublime artists of the Safavids, and the architects of the mighty palaces of Chosroes and the mosques of Esfahan (such as the Masjed-e Shah) and Mashhad that rank among the world's architectural marvels. In recent years, Iranian film-makers have won record numbers of international awards for their thoughtful and sometimes subtly subversive movies.

From Zoroaster to Muhammad

In many ways it is religion that has always been key to defining Iran's identity. It was in the 6th century B.C. that Cyrus the Great created one of the Ancient World's greatest empires, adopting Zoroastrianism as its official faith. Alexander the Great conquered Persia later in the 4th century B.C. but though he had vanquished its rulers, the state and its religion remained intact. When the Arabs embarked on their conquests of the Middle East and Mediterranean lands during the 7th century, Persia had become a decadent, crumbling edifice, like its great rival to the west, Byzantium.

Persia fell quickly to the Arabs and became part of the new Islamic empire. Its Zoroastrian ruling elite fled eastwards to India where their ancestors settled — there they are still known as the fire-worshipping Parsees. But Persia itself swiftly regained its individuality when many Muslims rejected the Sunnism of the Caliphs, the religious leaders who were the directly appointed successors of the Prophet Muhammad and who ruled with his authority. The Persians were prominent amongst those who chose instead to take their religious and political legitimacy from Ali, the fourth Caliph and the Prophet's son-in-law. They became known as the **Ahl-e Shi'a** or Shi'ites, the branch of Muslims found today not only in Iran and neighboring Iraq (Mesopotamia) but also countries such as Pakistan and North India. By breaking away in this way, Iran and its people once again managed to empower themselves politically while also maintaining their cultural distinctness.

This did not affect the unity of the Islamic world nor did it prevent Persia from continuing to play a leading role in this vast sphere of influence whose borders were spreading rapidly from Spain on the shores of the Atlantic in the west to the spice islands of Sumatra and beyond in the east. Prosperity and trade grew, with Persia benefiting from its geographical position at the centre of it all.

Such success, however, not only provoked conflict with the neighboring Christian empire of Byzantium but it also attracted the attention of new rivals from the plains and deserts of Central Asia. The following centuries saw waves of conquests by the Seljuk Turks and the Mongols, whose great generals were Genghiz Khan and Tamerlane the Great. But, just as had happened to the successors of Alexander the Great, these newcomers adopted the culture and even language of their new domain, and as each set up a new dynasty of rulers, golden ages of trade and culture followed each invasion of Persia — even if politically things did not.

The nation underwent a major revival under the Safavid dynasty (1502-1736), the most prominent figure of which was the supreme statesman Shah Abbas I. The wily general Nadir Shah and his successors followed, to be succeeded in turn by the Zand dynasty, founded by Karim Khan, and later the Qajars (1795-1925).

Era of the Peacock Throne

Just as revolution was in the air throughout Europe during the late 19th/early 20th centuries, 1905 saw a popular uprising against the ruling Shah, who was forced to hand over some of his power by allowing the country to become a constitutional monarchy in the following year. The discovery of oil in 1908 then ushered in another power-sharing problem when control of the region became fiercely disputed by the United Kingdom and Tsarist Russia.

As a consequence, World War I (1914-1918) gave Britain and Russia the excuse to occupy the country with the intention of ensuring stability in the region and to protect the oil fields. In 1919, Britain attempted to establish a protectorate in Iran, encouraged by the Soviet Union's withdrawal in 1921. Taking advantage of the uncertain situation, an ambitious cavalry officer Reza Khan led a coup that toppled the now impotent Qajars and installed himself in 1925 as the new Shah of his own Pahlavi dynasty. He brilliantly played the British at their own game and used the ever-increasing interest in his country by the superpowers to consolidate his position and to support his plan to modernize Iran.

World War II (1940-1945) saw Iran become a vital link in the Allies' supply line to the Soviet Union, circumventing the war fronts in Europe and North Africa. In August, 1941, British and Indian forces from Iraq and Soviet forces from the north occupied Iran, once again in the name of preserving regional stability. As a result, Reza abdicated in favor of his son Muhammad Reza Shah Pahlavi. In 1943 Tehran was a safe and logical place for the Allied leaders — Roosevelt, Churchill and Stalin — to hold a historic meeting that would not only determine the course of the war against Nazi Germany, Italy and Japan, but also redraw as much of the world map as they dared afterwards.

Although the Allied leaders had guaranteed Iran its post-war independence and boundaries, as soon as the war ended, Soviet troops stationed in northern Iran not only refused to withdraw but backed revolts that established short-lived republics in the province of Azerbaijan (populated by the Turkic Azerbaijanis in the north-west of Iran, bordering on today's Republic of Azerbaijan) and Iranian Kurdistan. The United States and the United Nations used diplomatic pressure backed by the promise (never honored) of oil concessions to force the Soviets to withdraw in 1946.

Hopes now rose that post-occupation Iran might become the constitutional monarchy that the people had struggled for ever since 1905. Shah Muhammad Reza at first held off from interfering with his government's decisions, but there was little he could do in any case to rectify the chronic instability caused by the West's interference during the immediate post-war years. Things came to a head when, in 1951, the prime minister Muhammad Mussadegh nationalized Iran's British-owned oil industry. This escalated into the Abadan Crisis (named after the oil port on the Persian Gulf), with the British imposing a economic blockade on the country. The Americans provided a solution by offering C.I.A. backing to the Shah who was then able to end the crisis by ousting Mussadegh.

Iran found itself facing new invaders, this time of a very different kind as it once again fell under the influence of the West who sought to control its vast oil reserves again for its own purposes. There was also another, more complex motive: the West was also seeking to control Iran in order to block the Soviet Union's own attempts to gain control there and to create a corridor to the Gulf for access to a "warm water port". The stand-off between the super-powers ominously echoed that of the 19th century when a similar push southwards by Tsarist Russia had been blocked by Britain and France.

In return for U.S. support to shore up his weakening position, the Shah agreed, in 1954, to allow an international consortium of British, American, Dutch and French and Dutch companies to run Iran's oil facilities for the next 25 years — but Iran would receive none of the billions of dollars of revenue generated. Stability, however, gradually returned in the late 1950s and 1960s and Iran was able to recommence its modernization of society and industry, fueled by the oil revenues from Iran's vast petroleum reserves — the third largest in the world — that were now flowing back into the country. But many Iranians felt that the Shah's liberal pro-Western policies were progressing too quickly and that, in any case, they were only enriching the country's elites.

From the mid-1960s onwards, the political situation became began to slide slowly back into instability. This encouraged the formation of a number of underground opposition organisations. The most prominent of these was the Mojahedin-e-Khalq (MEK), whose philosophy mixes Marxism and Islam and advocates the overthrow of the Iranian regime and its replacement with the group's own leadership. MEK orchestrated a wave of anti-Western attacks in the years leading up to the 1979 Islamic Revolution, after which it was expelled from Iran. The group then transferred its terrorist attacks against representatives of the new regime both in Iran and abroad; its primary support was provided by Iraq and its leader Saddam Hussein.

Seeds of revolution

After the assassination of president Hassan Ali Mansur in 1965, the Shah's secret service became more violently active. As in so many other Western-backed regimes throughout the rest of the world — particularly in Latin America — tens of thousands were arrested, tortured and killed. Understandably disillusioned with Western-style democracy, the opposition became polarised around the revolution-ary left-wing on the one hand, and around the Islamic clergy, headed by the Ayatollah Ruhollah Khomeini (who had been exiled in 1964), on the other.

Yet again oil proved a decisive factor in regional politics when relations with Iraq deteriorated, main-ly in clashes over the strategic Shatt al-Arab water-way which a Western-brokered agreement in 1937 had given to Iraq. Iran greatly increased its defense budget and by the early 1970s had become the region's strongest military power. In November, 1971 Iranian forces seized control of three islands at the mouth of the Persian Gulf. In response Iraq expelled thousands of ethnic Iranians who had lived peacefully within its borders.

In mid-1973, the Shah returned the oil industry to national control. Following the Arab-Israeli War of October, 1973, Iran did not join the Arab oil embar-go against the West and Israel. Instead it used the sit-uation to strengthen its ties with the West, while at the same time it cannily raised oil prices, using the profits for further modernization and to increase defense spending.

In the early 1970s, the Mojahedin had embarked

on a campaign aimed at assassinating Tehran-based U.S. military personnel and civilians involved in military contracts, seeking to weaken the regime and remove foreign influence. The institutionalised corruption of the Shah's regime and his U.S. backers had now succeeded in disaffecting the vast majority of the population, leading to widespread protests throughout the late 1970s. There was widespread religious as well as political opposition to the Shah's regime — a particular object of resentment was SAVAK, the hated internal security and intelligence service.

In September 1978, the government was forced to declare martial law, but it was too little too late. Reza was forced to flee into exile on January 16, 1979, never to return. Taking this as his cue, Khomeini promptly flew back from his own exile, and his opposition alliance overthrew the tottering government. Iran was declared a religious republic with Khomeini as its supreme leader. The Peacock Throne was no more.

In many respects the new government was ultra-conservative rather than religiously fundamentalist. Although it replaced Iran's modern Western-looking culture, laws and institutions with Islamic versions, it should be stressed that these were Shi'ite and Iranian in practise. Moreover, just as a secular government had done in the 1950s, industry was again nationalized to halt the damage caused by foreign influence.

There were further similarities as it soon became apparent that the new regime was determined to match the Shah in brutality and repression towards its citizens — in particular, the republic's new secret service was as feared as its predecessor SAVAK. Fiercely repressive measures were also taken against the different peoples of Iran, such as the Kurds, in a bid to ensure conformity to the new order. And yet the nation did not splinter. The West could barely hide its disappointment that civil war did not break out; instead, open opposition to the Ayatollahs of Khomeini's government mainly took the forms of clashes between rival religious factions.

War and revolt

The U.S. in particular was plunged into uncertainty over how to deal with the loss of its most prized ally (and its oil fields) in the Middle East. Paradoxically, it was the Iranians who provided an answer when militant students seized the U.S. embassy and its staff in Tehran on November 4, 1979, and held them hostage there until January 20, 1981. The Ayatollahs refused to intervene and President Jimmy Carter severed diplomatic relations and imposed economic sanctions on the country. In a bid to embarrass Carter in the eyes of the world, the hostages were deliberately released only after Carter lost the presidential elections to Ronald Reagan, who in turn had to disguise his humiliation at being forced to agree to the Iranian terms on the day of his inauguration. Although both sides claimed victory, it was clear that neither had won, and Iran was now fast becoming isolated from much of the international community as a result.

Covertly supported by the U.S., on September 22, 1980, Iraq invaded Iran, hoping to take advantage of its weakened state. Iran put its internal troubles aside and immediately rallied to fight back against these new invaders. But the bloody Iran-Iraq War resulted in a stalemate and continued until 1988, when both sides accepted a United Nations-brokered ceasefire. Ironically, the U.S. had all along been selling weapons to Iran as part of its shady Iran-Contra deals. The other countries of the West had also sold arms to both sides, quietly hedging their bets.

In 1981, a bomb exploded by the Mojahedin had killed 70 high-ranking Iranian officials, including the prime minister and president. Local resistance began to stir again in the regions and protest, though muted, began against the savage losses suffered at the war front. The combination of all this merely had the effect of strengthening Iran's government's stand against the West and its support for the (mainly Islamic) organisations that were increasingly carrying out attacks on Western-backed regimes in other countries. When the U.S. led the West's condemnation of Iran as a hotbed of terrorism, Iran's reply was to aim the same accusation at the U.S.

On the international front, the subsequent spiralling of incidents and misunderstandings worsened, serving only to focus on Iran the West's growing anti-Islamic attitudes. The U.S. led the boycott of trade with Iran while secretly breaking its own embargos, for example using neighboring Turkey as a middleman to buy Iranian oil. The U.S. used its barrage of accusations of international terrorism to reinforce its political clout in the Middle East, where Saudi Arabia had now replaced Iran as the U.S.'s most favored partner.

In general, Europe never sought to isolate Iran and so its inconsistency in supporting the U.S. has created only further rifts over how to deal with the beleaguered nation. Ironically, Russia has quietly sought to step into the U.S.'s shoes by making overtures to gain influence in Iran, but without much success.

This concerted assault on Iran by the West, supported by most regimes in the Arab world, has had the effect of holding back the democratic process in Iran. Iranians have been repeatedly forced to put their differences aside and unite to protect their homeland, in the process they have lost precious momentum in internal dialogue that could lead towards the democracy that the overwhelming majority desire.

The lessons of history have been ignored by the West: since time immemorial, Iranians have reserved the right to determine their own affairs. Patriotic to the last, they will defend even a tyrannical regime, particularly when faced with the more tyrannical option they see as being offered by the West.

Hopes for the future

After Khomeini's death in 1989, the pattern was now set of a nation split between a government seeking reform and democracy, and a clergy remaining ultra-conservative. Meanwhile, the opinions of the international community towards Iran continues to be divided, with many preferring to intrerpret Iran's right to act as a sovereign nation as a subversive act.

Despite such difficulties, Iran continues to keep the door open for dialogue with the West and also with the huge and vociferous expatriate community of Iranians throughout the world. Although Iranians, wherever they may be, may have problems with their rulers, they will always love their unique country and culture, of which they have every reason to be proud.

■ For further background information, see the Introduction to *Dari Dictionary & Phrasebook* (Hippocrene Books), and *The Iranians* (Bennett & Bloom, forthcoming).

A VERY BASIC GRAMMAR

—Structure
Like English, the linguistic structure of Farsi is refreshingly simple. In word order, the verb is usually put at the end of the sentence, e.g.

Shomâ telefun dârid?
"Do you have a telephone?"
(literally: "You telephone have?")

—Nouns
Farsi has no words for "the," "a" or "an" in the same way as English does — instead the meaning is generally undestood from the context, e.g. **doktur** can mean "the doctor," "a doctor" or just simply "doctor.'*

Nouns form their plural by simply adding **-ân** or **-hâ**, e.g. **zan** "woman" → **zan-ân** "women," **ruznâme** "newspaper" → **ruznâme-hâ** "newspapers". Although **-ân** is theoretically used for human plurals and **-hâ** for things, in everyday conversation they are more or less interchangeable.

There are some irregular plurals — analogous to examples in English like "man/men" or "child/children", e.g. **majles** "meeting" → **majâles** "meetings", **khat** "line" → **khotut** "lines", **salâh** "weapon" → **aslehâ** "weapons".

The genitive is formed using **-e/-ye,**** e.g. **mâshin-e mard** "the car of the man" or "the man's

---

* If you want to specifically emphasise "a" or "an" then you can use the word **yek** "a/an" or add **-i/-yi**, e.g. **yek doktur-i** "a doctor," **mardhâ-yi** "(some) men".
** This **e/ye** is called the **ezâfe**.

car," **shahr-e Tehrân** "the city of Tehran", **til-e petrôl** "gasoline" (literally: "oil of petrol"). For more on genitive constructions, see the sections on adjectives and possessives.

—Adjectives
These generally come after the noun and use the genitive **-e/-ye** as a connector, e.g.

"new" **nô** — **mâshin-e nô** "new car"
"old" **kohne** — **mâshin-e kohne** "old car"
Some other basic adjectives are:

open **bâz**	quick **tond**
shut **baste**	slow **yavâsh**
cheap **arzân**	big **bozorg**
expensive **gerân**	small **kuchek**
hot **garm**	old **pir; kohne***
cold **sard**	young **javân**
near **nazdik**	good **khob**
far **dur**	bad **bad**

Adding **bi-** to an existing noun gives the meaning of "without" or "-less", e.g. **taraf** "side" → **bitaraf** "neutral" (= "without side"), **kâr** "work" → **bikâr** "unemployed" (= "without work"), etc.

Most adjectives add **-tar** "-er", e.g. **kam** "little" → **kamtar** "less", **ziyâd** "much" → **ziyâdtar** "more".

—Adverbs
Most adverbs have a single form that does not change. Some examples:

here **injâ**	up **bâlâ**
there **ânjâ**	down **pâyin**
well **khob; khayr**	now **hâlâ**
badly **bad**	tomorrow **fardâ**

* **Pir** is used for people, **kohne** for things.

—Prepositions
Examples:

to **be; tâ**	with **bâ**
for **barâye; bare**	on **bâlâye; safe**
in **dar**	after **pas-e**
from **az**	in front of **pish-e**

e.g. **dar Irân** "in Iran," **az Ingilestân** "from England".

—Pronouns
Basic forms are as follows:

SINGULAR	PLURAL
I **man**	we **mâ**
you *singular* **tô**	you *plural* **shomâ**
he/she/it **u; ô**	they **ânhâ**

For "he/she/it" you will also find in formal or written Farsi the forms **in** ("this person") and **ân** ("that person"). Likewise for "they", where the alternatives are **inhâ**, **ânân** and **ishân**. In general, there is no change in meaning. Also use **shomâ** as the formal form of "you" for anyone you don't know well or who is older or more senior.

Possessive pronouns are:

SINGULAR	PLURAL
my **-am**	our **-emâ**
your **-et**	your **-etân**
his/her/its **-esh**	their **-eshân**

e.g. **mâshin-am** my car
     mâshin-esh his/her/its car
     mâshin-emâ our car

Simple demonstratives are:

this **in**	these **inhâ; inân**
that **ân**	those **ânhâ; ânân**

When these are used to modify a noun, you simply use the singular forms whether the noun is singular or plural, e.g. **in mard** "this man", **in mard-hâ** "these men", **ân zan** "that woman", **ân zan-ân** "those women".

—Verbs

Verbs are very easy to form, adding a number of prefixes and suffixes to the basic verb form. In fact the concept underlying the structure of Farsi verbs is so similar to those of the majority of European languages that its system of regularities and irregularities will soon appear quite familiar.

Every Farsi verb has a basic form that carries a basic meaning. To the end of this are added smaller words or single vowels that add further information to tell you who's doing what and how and when, e.g.

> **kharidan** "to buy"
> **kharidam** "I bought"
> **bekharam** "I may buy"
> **mikharam** "I am buying/will buy"
> **mikharidam** "I was buying"

Adding a form of the verb "to be" creates compound tenses, e.g. **kharida budam** "I had bought.' Some verbs, similar to European languages, have different stems for different tenses, e.g. **didan** "to see" → **didam** "I saw", **mibinam** "I see"; **goftan** "to speak" → **goftam** "I spoke", **miguyam** "I am speaking"; **âmadan** "to go" → **âmadam** "I went", but **mi'âyam** "I am going".

We saw the personal pronouns above, but these are only used for emphasis. Like French or Spanish, the verb already gives this information:

* The written forms are **-am**, **-at**, **-ash**.

SINGULAR	PLURAL
I **-am**	we **-in**
you *singular* **-i**	you *plural* **-id**
he/she/it **(-ad/-a)**	they **-an(d)**

e.g.

mikharam I buy	**mikharim** we buy
mikhari you buy	**mikharid** you buy
mikhare he/she/it buys	**mikharand** they buy

kharidam I bought	**kharidim** we bought
kharidi you bought	**kharidid** you bought
kharid he/she/it bought	**kharidand** they bought

You'll see that these are similar in form to the possessive pronouns on page 20.

"Not" is **ne/na**, e.g. **kharidam** "I bought" — **ne-kharidam** "I did not buy"; **estâd konid!** "stop!" — **estâd na-konid!** "don't stop!"

—Essential verbs

The verb "to be" is expressed in a variety of ways. The most common form you will find is the simple series of present endings for **budan**:

SINGULAR	PLURAL
hastam I am	**hastim** we are
hasti you are	**hastid** you are
has(t) he/she/it is	**hastand** they are

e.g. **Man doktur hastam.** "I am a doctor."

Although used slightly differently, the present tense of "to be" is contracted in a similar way to English (e.g. "I'm" for "I am", "she's" for "she is"):

SINGULAR	PLURAL
-am/-m I am	**-im** we are
-i you are	**-id** you are
-ast/-st he/she/it is	**-and/-nd** they are

e.g. **man âmada-m** "I am ready" (literally: "I ready am"), **ô chi-st?** "what is it?", **kojâ-st?** "where is (it)?"

"Is" can also be **e**, or **ye** if a vowel precedes it, e.g. **chi ye?** "what is it?", **Mâshin-man e.** "It's my car."

The negative forms are:

SINGULAR	PLURAL
nistam I am	**nistim** we are
nisti you are	**nistid** you are
nist he/she/it is	**nistand** they are

Past tense:

budam I was	**budim** we were
budi you were	**budid** you were
bud he/she/it was	**budand** they were

The verb "to have" is **dâshtan**:

SINGULAR	PLURAL
dâram I have	**dârim** we have
dâri you have	**dârid** you have
dâre he/she/it has	**dârand** they have

Examples:

Mâshin dâram. "I have a car."
Mâshin nadâram. "I don't have a car."
Nân dârid? "Do you have (any) bread?"
Chi kâr dârid? "What job do you do?"

Paralleling French, Italian and Spanish, this verb can be also used in the third person to express the sense of "there is/there are", e.g. **Nân dâra?** "Is there (any) bread?", **Khatar nadâra!** "There is no danger!'

"To want" is expressed using the verb **khâstan**, which has an irregular present form **khâh-**, e.g.

Man yek bilit be Tehrân mikhâham.
"I want a ticket to Tehran."

(literally: "I one ticket to Tehran want.")

"To like" is expressed in a similar way to French ("il me plaît") or Spanish ("me gusta"), using **dust dâshtan** "to please", e.g.

Man futbâl dust dâram.
"I like football."
Man futbâl dust nadâram.
"I don't like football."   ∎

PRONUNCIATION GUIDE

Farsi letter	Farsi example	Approximate English equivalent
a	**arusi** "wedding"	**a**pple
â	**âb** "water"	f**a**ther, as in South British English
b	**bale** "yes"	**b**ox
ch	**chây** "tea"	**ch**urch
d	**dokân** "shop"	**d**og
e	**esm** "name"	p**e**t
f	**futbâl** "soccer"	**f**at
g	**gâz** "gas"	**g**ot
gh	**gharb** "west"	*see page 26*
h	**hazâr** "thousand"	**h**at
i	**injâ** "here"	h**ea**t
j	**jahân** "world"	**j**et
k	**kuchek** "small"	**k**ick
kh	**khôsh-hâl** "happy"	lo**ch**, as in Scottish English
l	**lotfan** "please"	**l**et
m	**mâshin** "car"	**m**at
n	**nân** "bread"	**n**et
o	**otâgh** "room"	c**o**t, as in British English
ô	**dô** "two"	c**oa**t
p	**polis** "police"	**p**et
r	**râdyô** "radio"	**r**at, but "rolled" as in Scottish English
s	**sinamâ** "cinema"	**s**it
sh	**shahr** "town"	**sh**ut
t	**taksi** "taxi"	**t**en
u	**pul** "money"	sh**oo**t
v	**vaght** "time"	**w**orld
y	**yakh** "ice"	**y**es
z	**zelzele** "earthquake"	**z**ebra
zh	**rezhim** "regime"	era**z**ure
'	**ma'nâ** "meaning"	*see page 26*

Nothing beats listening to a native speaker, but the following notes should help give you some idea of how to pronounce the following letters.

Like English, the spoken language has a range of variations in pronunciation that are not always reflected in the written language. Most of the language in this book, however, is deliberately close to the written language thus enabling you to be understood clearly wherever you may be.

—Vowels
The combination **ay** is pronounced as the "y" in English "wh**y**", e.g. **khayli** "very".

—Consonants

kh is the rasping "ch" in Sottish "loch" and German "ach", frequently transcribed in English as "kh". It is also pronounced like the Castillian Spanish "jota".

r varies between two forms: from the rolled Scottish variant to a lightly breathed tap of the tongue that sometimes sounds similar to **zh**. This is the same **r** found in Turkish.

' represents the same pronunciation of two underlying sounds: the "glottal stop" — a simple stop of the breath instead of a consonant — or a representation of the pharyngal consonant ^c*ain* found in words of Arabic origin (it also occurs in Aramaic and classical Hebrew). In Farsi, when it comes before a consonant, it prolongs the preceding vowel, sometimes with a slight "creak" of breath separating the two, e.g. **ma'nâ** "meaning" is pronounced "**ma'anâ**" or more usually "**mânâ**", **she'r** "poem" as "**she'er**". When it comes after a consonant, it is usually pronounced as a sort of stop or catch in the flow of breath before articulating the following vowel, e.g. **san'at** "industry" is pronounced in two distinct segments as "san-at". [equivalent to Turkish ']

gh is pronounced like a sort of growl in the back of your throat — like when you're gargling. Frequently written in English as "gh" when transcribing other languages that have this sound, the German or Parisian "r" is the easy European equivalent. Note that it represents the same pronunciation of two underlying sounds, **ghayn** [غ] and **ghâf** (**qâf**) [ق], which many speakers may emphasize especially for religious reasons (they are two distinct sounds in the Arabic of the Qur'an) or for dialectical reasons.

—Spelling notes

1) Like English, there are variants in the pronunciation of spoken language that are not reflected in the spelling, most importantly you will hear **u** for **â**, e.g. "**Tehrun**" for **Tehrân**, "**jun**" for **jân** "dear".

2) In the rare cases where the letters **sh** represent the two separate sounds **s** and **h** in sequence, they are divided by an hyphen, e.g. **Es-hâq** "Isaac". Likewise for **z** and **h** to distinguish the sequence from the single sound **zh**, e.g. **maz-hab** "sect" or "religion".

3) Remember that **h**, as a separate letter, is always pronounced in combinations like **mashhur** ("**mash-hur**") "famous", **solh** ("**sol-h**") "peace."

4) Many Farsi words are spelt with doubled consonants. Because this simply reflects the established spelling conventions in Farsi script and has no effect on pronunciation, the transliteration used in this book uses only single letters (e.g. **motashakker-am!** "thank you!" is written as **motashaker-am!**) ■

The Farsi alphabet

Farsi letter	Roman equivalent	Name of letter	Farsi letter	Roman Equivalent	Name of letter
ا، آ	a, â	alef	ض	z	zâd
ب	b	be	ط	t	tâ
پ	p	pe	ظ	z	zâ
ت	t	te	ع	'	ayn
ث	s	se	غ	gh	ghayn
ج	j	jim	ف	f	fe
چ	ch	che	ق	gh	ghâf
ح	h	he-ye hoti	ک	k	kâf
خ	kh	khe	گ	g	gâf
د	d	dâl	ل	l	lâm
ذ	z	zâl	م	m	mim
ر	r	re	ن	n	nun
ز	z	ze	و	v, u, ô	vâv
ژ	zh	zhe	ه	h	he-ye dô chesm
س	s	sin	ی	y, i	ye
ش	sh	shin			
ص	s	sâd	ء	'	hamze

NOTES
1. Note that the short vowels **a**, **e**, and **o** are not normally written.
2. **Ayn** and **hamze** are not always written in the transliteration used in this book.

Numbers

٠	١	٢	٣	٤\٣	٥	٦	٧	٨	٩	١٠
0	**1**	**2**	**3**	**4***	**5**	**6**	**7**	**8**	**9**	**10**

* The two forms for 4
are interchangeable.

FARSI
Dictionary

FARSI–ENGLISH
FARSI–INGILISI

A/A

âb water; âb khordan drinking water; âb mive fruit juice; âb nabât candy; âb o havâ climate; âb shâr waterfall; âb shodan to thaw; âb-e dehan saliva; âb-e garm hot water; âb-e gusht gravy; âb-e jô beer; âb-e ma'dani mineral water; âb-e sard cold water

Âbân *name of the 8th Iranian month*

âbi blue

âbkesh sieve

abr cloud

abri cloudy

abrisham silk

abrishami silken

âbroft landslide

abru eyebrow

âbyâri irrigation

âchâr spanner/wrench

adab courtesy

adabiyât literature

âdam person; âdam-e tab'idi displaced person; âdam-hâ-ye tab'idi displaced persons

adâme dâdan to continue

âdamkosh killer

âdâms chewing gum

adâptar adapter

adas lentils

âdres address

adviye spice

Afghânestân Afghanistan

Afghâni Afghani

afsar officer

afshândan to sow

âftâb sun; Âftâbi miyâd. It is sunny.

afzâr tools

Âghâ Mr.

aghab backwards; aghab neshini kardan to retreat

aghaliyat minority; aghaliyat-e nezhâdi ethnic minority

âghâ-ye mosen *male* old person

aghrab scorpion

âhan iron

âhangar locksmith

ahâte kardan to surround

Ahl-e Vaylz Welsh

ahram crowbar

âhu deer

ajale hurry; Ajale dâram. I am in a hurry.

âjor brick

akâdemi academy

âkhar end

âkhari last

aks var dâri photography

aksariyat majority

âksizhen oxygen

al'ân now

alaf-e khoshk hay

alangu bangle

âlât-e tanâsoli genitals

âlbâlu morello cherry

Âlemâni German

Âlmân Germany

âlu plum
amâ but
âmadan to come
amaliyât; amal (act of) surgery
âmbulâns ambulance
amniyat safety; security
Âmrikâ America; U.S.A.
Âmrikâ'i American
ân that; **ân chi-ye?** what's that?; **ân var** that way
anâr pomegranate
andâkhtan to throw
andâm-hâ limbs
andâze size
ânfluyenzâ flu
angosht finger; **angosht-hâ** fingers; **angosht-e neshân** index finger; **angosht-e pâ** toe
angoshtâne thimble
angur grape(s)
ânhâ they; those
ânjâ there
anjir fig
anjoman assembly; meeting
ankabut spider
âns ounce
ântibiyotik antibiotic
âpârtemân apartment
Arab Arab
Arâgh Iraq
Arâghi Iraqi
ârd flour
are saw
ârenj elbow
Armanestân Armenia
Armani Armenian
artesh army; **artesh-e daryâ'i** navy
arusi wedding
arz foreign exchange/currency

arzan millet
arzân cheap
asâ stick; walking stick
asab nerve
asal honey
âsân easy
âsânsur lift/elevator
âsâr monument; ruins
asb horse; **asb-e nar** stallion; **asb davâni** horse racing; **asb savâri** horseback riding; **asb ve gâri** horse and cart
âsemân sky
âshpazi kardan to cook
asir prisoner; **asir-e jangi** prisoner-of-war; **asir kardan** prisoner: to take prisoner
aslahe weapon; arms; **aslahe-ye zed-e havâ'i** anti-aircraft gun
âspirin aspirin
asr evening; in the evening
âsyâb mill; **âsyâb kardan** to grind
âtesh fire
âteshbas ceasefire
atr perfume; deodorant
aval first
Âvril April
âyande future
aydz AIDS
âyene mirror
ayker acre
aynak glasses; eyeglasses; **aynak âftâbi** sunglasses
az from; by; **az bar yâd gereftan** to learn by heart
âzâd free; **âzâd kardan** to free
âzâdi freedom
Âzar *name of the 9th Iranian month*

Âzarbâyjân Azerbaijan
Âzarbâyjâni Azerbaijani
âzemun test; âzemun kar-
   dan to test
âzhâns agency; âzhâns-e
   emdâd aid agency;
   âzhâns-e mosâferat travel agency
âzhendâ agenda
azule muscle

B

bâ with; bâ yakh, lotfan
   with ice, please
ba'd az zohr afternoon; in
   the afternoon
ba'di next
bache child; infant; bache-
   hâ children; bache nô-
   zâd newborn child
bad bad
bâd wind; Bâd miyâd. It is
   windy.
bâdâm almond
badan body
bâdemjân aubergine; egg-
   plant
bagâzh bags; baggage
bâgh garden; bâgh-e mive
   orchard; bâgh-e vahsh
   zoo
bahâr spring
bahman avalanche; Bah-
   man name of the 11th
   Iranian month
bahs discussion
bâlâ top; up; bâlâ-ye on
baladan to speak; (Âyâ)
   shomâ Fârsi baladid? Do
   you speak Farsi?; Man
   Fârsi baladam. I speak
   Farsi.
baldarchin quail

bale yes
bâlesht pillow
balkon balcony
Baluch Baluchi
bâm roof
bâmiye okra; lady's fingers
banafsh purple
bând bandage
bândâzh dressing medical
band-e nâf umbilical cord
bânk bank
bânkdâr banker
bâr baggage; bar; bâr-e
   ezâfe excess baggage
barâdar brother
bârân rain; Bârân miyâd. It
   is raining.
bârâni raincoat
barâ-ye; bare for
bardâshtan to pick up
bare lamb
barf snow; barf kuri snowblindness; Barf miyâd It
   is snowing.; barf pâk-
   kon windscreen wipers
barg leaf
bargh electricity; lightning
bârik narrow
Baritânyâ Britain
barnâme (-e kâmpyuter)
   (computer) program
bas enough; bas ast! that's
   enough!
bâsan bottom
bâsketbâl basketball
bastani ice-cream
bâstâni archeological
baste closed; parcel
bâtri battery
bayât: nân-e bayât stale
   bread
bâz open; hawk
bâzâr market; bâzâr yâbi
   marketing

be to; with; at; **Be penisilin hasâsiyat dâram.** I'm allergic to penicillin.

bebakhshid! excuse me!

bedehkâri debt

bedun-e without; **bedun-e yakh, lotfan** no ice, please; **bedun-e shekar, lotfan!** no sugar, please!

befârma'id! come in!; please!; come to the table!; please eat!; you're welcome!; **befarmâ'id, beshinid!** please sit down!

behtar better

benzin petrol

berenj *uncooked* rice

berger burger

berid! go!

bi without; -less **bi maze** tasteless

bidâr shodan to wake up

bihâsel barren *land*

bil spade

bime insurance

bimârestân hospital; **bimârestân-e hâmele** maternity hospital

bimâri illness; disease; **bimâri-ye ertefâ** altitude sickness

bime insurance.

binâyi eyesight

bini nose

birun outside

bisavâd illiterate

bishtar more

bist twenty

bistom twentieth

bitarbiyat rude

bohrân crisis

boland high; tall

bolbol nightingale

bolur crystal

boluz jumper/sweater

bômb bomb; **bômb-e khoshe'i** cluster bomb; **bômb-e monfajer nashode** unexploded bomb

bômbarân kardan to bomb

bordan to win

boridan to cut

borj tower

borôs brush; hairbrush

boshghâb plate

boshke-ye mohemât gun barrel

botri-ye âb water bottle

boz goat

bozorg big

budan to be

buf owl

bufâlô buffalo

bukhâri heater; stove

bu smell; **bu dâdan** to smell **bu kardan** to smell *something*

CH

châdor chador; veil; tent

châghu knife; **châghu-ye kuchek-e jibi** penknife

châh well (of water)

chahârdah fourteen

chahâr four; **chahâr-râh** crossroads; **chahâr pâyân-e asli** livestock

chahârom fourth

Chahârshambe Wednesday

chakme boot(s)

chakosh hammer

chaman grass

chamedân suitcase

chand? how much *(price)*?; **chand (tâ)?** how many?

châne chin

changâl fork
chap left
chapi left-wing
châr four
charbi fat
charm leather
chasp glue; plaster/Bandaid
chatr umbrella; parasol
chây tea; **chây bâ limu** tea with lemon; **chây bâ shir** tea with milk; **chây bidun-e shir** tea without milk
châykhâne teahouse
che? what?; **cheturi?/che juri?** how?
cheghadr? how much?; **cheghadr nazdik?** how near?; **cheghadr dur?** how far?
chehel forty
chek-in check-in
cherâ? why?
cherâgh light; lamp; cooker/stove; **cherâgh ghove** flashlight
cherik guerrilla
cheshâyi taste
cheshm eye; **cheshm-hâ** eyes; **cheshm-e masnu'i** artifical eye
chetur? how?; **chetur-i(d)?** how are you?
chi? what?
Chin China
Chini Chinese
choghondar beetroot
chub wood; **chub dasti** crutch

D
dâdan to give
dâdgâh law court

daftar office; **daftar-e etelâ'ât** information office
daftarche notebook; exercise book
dâgh hot
daghighe minute
dah ten
dahom tenth
dalil reason; **dalil-e safar** reason for travel
damâgh nose
dâmane slope; **dâmane-ye kuh** foothills
damâsanj thermometer
dam-e cheragh ghermez at the traffic lights
dampâ'i *flipflops*
dandân tooth; **dandân-hâ** teeth; **dandân dard** toothache; **dandân pezeshk/dandân-sâz** dentist; **dandân-forush** dentist's surgery
dande gear; rib; **dande-hâ** ribs; **dande aghab** reverse gear; **dande-ye khalâs** neutral drive
dâneshgâh university
dâneshju *university* student
dâneshmand scientist
dânestan to know
dane-ye barf snowflakes
dar in; **dar bâz-kon** bottle-opener/corkscrew
dâr door
daraje thermometer
darband ravine
darbâz kon can opener
dard pain
dare valley; **dare-tand** ravine
darô kardan to reap
dars lesson
dâru *medical* drug

dârukhâne chemist's/pharmacy

daryâche lake

dasht plain/plains

dâshtan to have

dast hand; arm; **dast-e chap** left/left-hand; **dast-e râst** right/right-hand; **dast-e chap bepich** turn left; **dast-e râst bepich** turn right; **dast-e masnu'i** artifical arm

dastband bracelet

dastgâh apparatus; **dastgâh-e di-vi-di** D.V.D. player; **dastgâh-e fâks** fax machine; **dastgâh-e fotokopi** photocopier; **dastgâh-e si-di** C.D. player

dastgir handle; **dastgir kardan** to arrest

dastkesh gloves

dastmâl handkerchief; napkin; **dastmâl kâghazi** tissues; **dastmâl tuvâlet** toilet paper

dastur zabân grammar

davâ *medical* drug; **davâ-ye bihushi** anesthetic; **davâ-ye pashe** insect repellant

dâvar referee

dâvatalab volunteer

davâzdah twelve

davidan to run

Day *name of the 10th Iranian month*

deh village

dehan mouth

deldard stomachache

demôkrâsi democracy

derakht tree

Desambr December

deser dessert

didan to see

digar other; **yek shishe-ye digar** another bottle

dijitâl digital

diktâtôr dictator

diktâtôri dictatorship

din religion

diplumât diplomat

diruz yesterday; **diruz sobh** yesterday morning; **diruz ba'd az zohr** yesterday afternoon

dishab last night

diskô disco; nightclub

divâr wall

di-vi-di D.V.D.

dô two; **dô hafte** fortnight; **dô sâl dige** the year after next; **dô sevom** two-thirds; **dô-shâkhe** (two-pin electric) plug; **dô-charkhe** bicycle; **dô-ghulu** twins

dôbâr twice

dôkân shop

dokhtar daughter; girl; **dokhtar bache** baby girl

dokme button

doktur-e atfâl pediatrician

doktur-e pezeshk doctor

dolâr dollar

dôlat nation; state

dôre-ye dah sâleh decade

dorost true

dorugh lie

Dôshambe Monday

doshman enemy

dôvom second

dozd! thief!

dozdi robbery; theft

dur far

durbin binoculars; camera

dush shower

dushidan to milk *an animal*
dust friend; **dust dâshtan** to love; to like

E

-e/-ye of
ech-ây-vi HIV
edâre office; **edâre-ye forush-e bilit** ticket office
eghâmatgâh hostel; accommodation
ehtiyâj need
ejtehâd *noun* struggle
ekzâst exhaust
e'lânât advertising
emâm imam
emkânât facilities; **Emkânât dârid barâye ma'alulin?** Do you have facilities for the disabled?
emruz today; **emruz sobh** this morning; **emruz ba'd az zohr** this afternoon; **emruz asri** this evening
emsâl this year
emshab tonight
emtehân test; exam; **emtehân kardan** to test
emzâ signature
enghelâb revolution
enteghâl-e khun blood transfusion
entekhâb kardan to choose
entekhâbât election(s)
ertebât communications
Esfand *name of the 12th Iranian month*
esfânj sponge
esfenâj spinach
es-hâl diarrhea; **es-hâl khuni** dysentery
eshtebâh: Eshtebâh mikonid. You are wrong.
eshtehâ appetite

eskaner scanner
Eskâtland Scotland
Eskâtlandi Scottish
eskenâs-e banki bank notes
eski skiing
Eslâm Islam
Eslâmi Islamic
esm name; **esm-e fâmil** surname; **esm-e vasati** middle name
Espâniyâ Spain
Espâniyâ'i Spanish
Esrâ'ili Israeli
estadyum stadium
estefâr kardan to camouflage
estefrâgh kardan to vomit
esteghâmat kardan to resist
esteghlâl independence
estekân tea-glass
estishan train station
etehâdiye-ye asnâf trade union
etelâ'ât information
e'terâz *noun* protest
e'tiyâdi be alkol alcoholism
ezâfe extra

F

fahmidan to understand
fajr dawn
fak jaw
fâks fax
fâkulti faculty
fâmil relative
Farânsavi French
fardâ tomorrow; **fardâ sobh** tomorrow morning; **fardâ ba'd az zohr** tomorrow afternoon; **fardâ shab** tomorrow night
farhang dictionary; culture

farmân steering wheel; **farmân dâdan** to command
farsh carpet *knotted*
Farvardin *name of the 1st Iranian month*
fasl season
fâynal final
felâsh flash
felez metal
felfel pepper(s); **felfel dolmeyi** sweet pepper(s)
fenjân cup
fer-e khorâk pazi stove: *cooking*
fesâd corruption
feshâr pressure; **feshâr-e khun** blood pressure; **feshâr-e bâlâ** high blood pressure; **feshâr-e pâ'in** low blood pressure
Fevriye February
fighra vertebra
fil elephant
film film; **film-e rangi** color film; **film-se siyâh o sefid** black and white film
filmsâz film-maker
fishang cartridge *for gun*
fiziyoterâpi physiotherapy
forudgâh airport
forushendagi sales
forushgâh store; shop; **forushgâh-e lavâzem-e tahrir** stationer's
fotokopi photocopy
fulâd steel
fut foot
futbol soccer/football

G/GH
gach chalk
gale flock; herd; **gale-ye gâv** cattle
gâleri gallery; **gâleri-ye honari** art gallery
gâlôn gallon
gandom wheat; **gandom-e siyâh** rye
gardan neck
gardanband necklace
gâri carriage
garm hot; warm
garmâ-ye fôghul'âde heatwave
gasht patrol
gâv cow; **gâv-e nar** bull; **gâv-e âhan** plow
gavazn deer; antelope; **gavazn-e nar** stag
gâz gas; accelerator; cooker/stove
gelâs glass
gelim kilim; rug
gelu throat
gerân expensive
gerdu walnut
gereftan to get; to take; to learn
gerepfrut grapefruit
gerôgân hostage
ghâbela midwife
ghabrestân cemetery
ghabul shodan to pass *an exam*
ghad extent; **ghad boland** tall; **ghad kutâh** short
ghadam zadan to walk
ghadimi ancient
ghafase cupboard; **ghafase-ye sine** ribcage
ghaht famine
ghahve coffee; **ghahve bâ shir** coffee with milk
ghahve'i brown
ghalam pen; **ghalam-e mu**

brush
ghalb heart
ghale corn; summit
ghal'e castle; fort
ghâleb shodan (bar) to conquer
ghâli; ghâliche rug
ghand sugarlump
ghânun law
ghâr cave
gharârdâd-e bime insurance policy
ghârat kardan to loot
gharb west
gharghâvol pheasant
gharn century
gharz debt
ghasaba ar-ri'a trachea
ghasaba'i kubrâ tibia
ghasâbi butcher's shop
ghâshogh spoon; **ghâshogh chây khuri** teaspoon
ghat'-e andâm kardan to amputate
ghâtel killer
ghâter mule
ghatl murder
ghavi strong
ghaychi scissors
ghâyegh boat
ghâz goose
ghazâ food; meal; provisions; **ghazâ-hâ** meals
ghazâl gazelle
ghâzi judge
ghermez red
ghesmat-e bâr baggage counter
ghofl lock; padlock; **ghofl-e dâr** doorlock
ghors-e khâb sleeping pill
ghors-e mâh full moon
ghorub evening; **ghorub-e**

âftâb sunset
ghotbnamâ compass
ghuch ram
ghurbâghe frog
ghuri teapot
ghuti can; **ghuti-ye rôghan** oilcan
ghuyud airdrop
ghuzak ankle
gilâs cherry
gire-ye châdor tent pegs
gishniz coriander
giyâh plant
gôje farangi tomato
gol goal; rose; **gol-forush** florist; **gol kalam** cauliflower
golâbi pear
goldân vase
golule bullet
gom kardan to lose
gomrok customs
gonjeshk sparrow
gorâz boar
gorbe cat
gorg wolf
Gorjestân Georgia
Gorjestâni Georgian
gorosne hungry; **Man gorosne hastam.** I'm hungry.
govâhi dâdan to testify
gozâresh report
gozargâh-e kuhi mountain pass
gozashte past
grâm gram
grup-e khun blood group
gune cheek
guni sack
gur tomb; **gur-e moghadas** saint's tomb
gusâle calf

gusfand sheep
gush ear; gush-hâ ears
gushe corner
gushi handset; gushi-ye tebi stethoscope
gusht meat; gusht-e bare lamb; gusht-e boz goat; gusht-e gâv beef; gusht-e gusfand mutton
gushvâre earrings

H

haft seven
haftâd seventy
hafte week; hafte-ye gozashte last week; in hafte this week; hafte-ye dige next week
haftom seventh
haghighat truth
hâlâ now
halazun snail
hâl-e hâzer present
halghe ring
ham also
hamâm bathroom
hâmele pregnant; Man hâmele hastam. I'm pregnant.
hamin al'ân just now
hamkâr colleague
haml: vaz'-e haml childbirth; haml kardan to carry
hamle assault; attack; hamle-ye havâ'i air-raid
hamsafar *traveling* companion
hang regiment
harârat speed
harekat movement; harekat nakonid! don't move!
harf zadan to speak

hâri rabies
hasâsiyat allergy
hâselkhiz fertile
hashare insect; hasharât insects; hashare kosh insect repellant; insecticide
hasht eight
hashtâd eighty
hashtom eighth
hast? is there?
hastand? are there?
havâ air; weather
havâkesh fan
havânavardi aviation
havâpaymâ airplane
havich carrots
havu co-wife
hayvân animal; hayvânât animals
hâzer ready; Hâzer am. I am ready.
hediye gift
hefz memory; care; hefz-o-seha hygiene
helâl crescent; helâl-e mâh new moon; Helâl-e Ahmar Red Crescent
helikopter helicopter
hendevâne watermelon
Hendi Indian
Hendu Hindu
Hendustân India
hepâtit hepatitis
hesâb sum; bill
hesâbdâr accountant
hezâr thousand
hezb (-e siyâsi) (political) party
hijdah eighteen
hivdah seventeen
hizom firewood
hoghugh right(s); hoghugh-e bashar human rights; hoghugh-e madani civil

rights
hokumat government
Holândi Dutch
hôle towel
holu peach
hostel hostel
hotel hotel
hôz pond

I

imayl e-mail
in this; **in var** this way; **in hafte** this week
Ingilis Britain; England
Ingilisi British; English
inhâ these
injâ here; **injâ-st** here is ...; **injâ-nd** here are ...
internet internet
Irân Iran
Irâni Iranian *person*
Irland Ireland; **Irland-e Shomâli** Northern Ireland
Irlandi Irish
ishân they
istâdan to stand
istgâh station; **istgâh-e polis** police station; **istgâh-e otobus** bus station; bus stop; **istgâh-e ghatâr** railway station; **istgâh-e bâzrasi-ye marz** checkpoint
Italiyâ Italy
Italiyâ'i Italian

J

jâ place; **jâ-ye châdor zadan** campsite
ja'be box
jâde road; **jâde-ye âsfâlt** tarmac road

jadval-e safar timetable
jâk jack
jalase session
jam' addition; **jam' kardan** to add
jan pâk sanitary towels
jânevar bug/insect
jang war; **jang-e dâkheli** civil war
jangal wood; forest
jangande fighter *soldier*
jarâh surgeon
jâsus spy
javâb answer
javâher jewelry
javân young
javâri corn
jâz jazz
jehâd jihad
jehângardi travel
jelighe waistcoat *jacket without sleeves*
jelô forwards; in front of
jenâh râst right-wing
jenâyat crime
jenâyatkâr criminal
jib pocket
jigar liver
jinz jeans
jip 4-wheel drive
jirjirak cricket *(insect)*
jô barley
joft placenta
joghrâfi geography
jôhar ink
Jom'e Friday; **masjed-e Jom'e** Friday mosque
jomjome skull
jonub south
jorm crime
jurâb socks; **jurâb shalvâri** tights/pantyhose
jush spot *on skin*
juy-e âb stream

kabâb

K/KH

kabâb kebab
kâbine cabinet
kabk partridge
kâbl cable
kabutar dove; pigeon
kachâlu sweet potato/sweet potatoes
kâdô present; gift
kadu tanbel pumpkin
kaf: kaf-e dast palm *of hand*; **kaf-e pâ** sole *of foot*
kafe café; **kafe internet** internet café
kâfi enough
kafsh(-ha) shoe(s); **kafsh forushi** shoeshop
kaftar pigeon
kâghaz paper; **kâghaz barâye neveshtan** writing paper
kâh straw
kahdân barn
kahrabâ amber
kâhu lettuce
kalâch clutch
kalâgh crow
kalam cabbage
kâlej college
kam little; very little; not enough; **yek kam** a little bit; **kam âbi** dehydration; **kam khuni** anemia
kamar waist; **kamar dard** backache
kamarband belt
kambâyn combine harvester
kamin ambush
kâmp-e panâhandegân refugee camp
kâmpyuter computer; I.T.
kamtar less
kâmyon truck/lorry

Kânâdâ Canada
Kânâdâ'i Canadian
kânâl canal
kane tick *insect*
kânfarâns conference
kânsert concert
kâpi copy; **kâpi kardan** to copy
kâpsul-e gâz gas canister
kâput bonnet/hood; condom
kâr work; **kâr kardan** to work
kârd knife
kare butter
kârgar factory worker; **kârgar-e emdâdi** aid worker
kârmand office worker; official; **kârmand-e dawlat** civil servant; **kârmand-e emdâdi** relief worker
kârt card; **kârt postâl** postcard; **kârt-e e'tebâr** credit card; **kârt-e savâr shodan** boarding pass; **kârt postâl** postcard
kârvân convoy
kâse bowl; **kâse-ye sar** skull
kâseb business person
kaset cassette; **kaset vidyô** videotape
kâshtan to plant; to grow
kasif dirty
Kâtulik Catholic
kay? when?
kayk; kek flea
kayki shirini cake
kelâs class
kelid key
kelisâ church
kerâvât tie; necktie
kerm worm; **kerm-e abrisham** silkworm(s); **kerm-e sad-pâ** caterpillar;

khormâ

kerm-e shab tâb firefly
keshâvarz farmer
keshâvarzi agriculture; farming; agriculture; **keshâvarzi shenâs** agronomist
keshmesh raisins
keshô drawer
kesht kardan to cultivate
keshti ferry
keshvar-e mostaghel independent state
ketâb book; **ketâb-e râhnamâ** guidebook; **ketâbforushi** bookshop/bookstore
ketâbkhâne library
ketri kettle
khâb sleep; **...-am khâb rafte.** I have pins and needles in my ...
khabar-negâr journalist
khâbidan to sleep
khafe shodan choke; **Khafe mishavad!** He/She is choking!
khâhar sister
khâhesh mikonam! please!
khâk soil; earth
khâkastari grey
khalabân pilot
khalâl dandân toothpick
khalebân pilot
khâli empty
khâm raw
khamir dandân toothpaste
khânavâde family
khândan to read
khâne house; **khâne âbâd!** may your home be forever!
khanjar dagger
khânom wife; **Khânom** Mrs.; Miss; **khânom-e mosen**

old person *female*
khar donkey
kharâb bad; spoiled; badly; **kharâb kardan** to destroy
kharboze melon
kharchang crab
khardal mustard
khargush rabbit
kharid shopping
kharman harvest
khârposht hedgehog
khâstan to want
khat line
khatar danger; **khatar!** danger!
khatkesh ruler *instrument*
khatne circumcision
khâvyâr caviar; **mâhi-ye khâvyâr** sturgeon
khayat dressmaker; tailor
khayli very; too; **khayli sard** very cold; **khayli garm** very hot; **khayli mamnun!** thank you
khazâne treasury
khers bear
khiyâbân road; street; **khiyâbân-e yek tarafe** one-way street
khiyâr cucumber
khob good; well; fine; **khob!** well!; okay!
khod mokhtâri autonomy
khodâ hâfez! goodbye!
khodkâr pen
khofâsh bat
khompâre mortar; shell
khonak cool
khorâk dâdan to feed an animal
Khordad *name of the 3rd Iranian month*
khordan to eat
khormâ dates(s)

khoruj exit; departures; **khoruj-e ezterâri** emergency exit

khorus cockerel/rooster

khosh: khosh-hâl happy; **khosh âmadid!** welcome!; **khosh maze** tasty

khoshk dry; barren *land*; **khoshk sâli** drought; **khoshk-shu'i** laundry

khoshunat violence

khuk pig

khun blood

ki? who?

kif bag; handbag; **kif-e pul** wallet; **kif-e madrase** satchel

kilogrâm kilogram

kilometr kilometer

Kirghiz Kirgiz

Kirghizestân Kirgizstan

kise bag; **kise khâb** sleeping bag; **kise-ye sofrâ** gall bladder

klinik clinic

kodâm? which?

kohne old

kojâ? where?; **kojâ-st?** where is?; **kojâ-nd?** where are?

kolâh hat

kolang pickaxe

kolerâ cholera

kolye kidney

komak help; **komak!** help!; **komak kardan** to help; **komak-e emdâdi** relief aid; **komak-e ensâni** humanitarian aid; **Man-ô komak konid!** Help me!

komisyun commission

konsulgari consulate

konyâk brandy

Kord Kurd

kore-ye asb pony

korsi seat; stool

koshtan to kill

koshtar-e nezhâdi ethnic cleansing

koshti wrestling

kôt jacket; **kôt-o-shalvâr** suit

krem cream; ointment; **krem-e rish** shaving cream; **krem-e âftâb gereftan** sunblock cream

kriket cricket

kristâl crystal

kuche sidestreet

kuchek small

kud fertilizer; manure

kudak infant

kudetâ coup d'etat

kuh mountain

kul-e poshti backpack; rucksack

kune-ye tofang butt *of rifle*

kurmush mole *animal*

kusan cushion *small*

kushesh *noun* struggle

kutâh low; short

kuzeh pot

kuzehgari pottery

kyosk kiosk; **kyosk-e ruznâme** newsstand

L

lab lip

labaniyât dairy

lab-e rudkhâne river bank

lâk nail polish

lâmp lightbulb

lashkar troops; **lashkar-e hâfez solh** peace-keeping troops

lâshkhur vulture

lâstik rubber; tyre/tire

lavâzem: lavâzem-e ârâyesh toiletries; **lavâzem-e film-vardâri** camera equipment; **lavâzem-e tahrir** stationery
lebâs clothes; dress; **lebâs-forushi** clothes shop
lenz contact lenses; lens
limu lemon; **limu sabz** lime
litr liter
livân glass; **yek livân âb** a glass of water
lôh slate
lotfan please; **Lotfan muhâm-râ bezanid.** I'd like a haircut please.
lôz-ul-me'de pancreas
lubiyâ beans
lule tube; **lule-ye dâkheli** inner tube

M

mâ we
ma'alul disabled person; **ma'alulin** disabled people
ma'bad temple
madâd pencil; **madâd sham'i** crayon
madâdkâr aid worker
mâdar mother; **mâdar bozorg** grandmother
madârek-e mâshin car papers
mâdiyân mare
madrase school; madrasa
mafsal joint; **mafsal-e rân** hip; **mafsal-hâ-ye rân** hips
magas fly
maghâle article
maghâze shop/store
maghsud objective

maghz brain
mâh month; moon
mahal place; **mahal-e taval-od** place of birth
mahali local; **dôkân-e mahali barâ-ye mardom-e mahali** a local shop for local people
mâhi fish; **sag-e mâhi; mâhi-ye khâvyâr** sturgeon
mahkum kardan to con-demn
mahsul crops
majale magazine
majles parliament; **majles-e bâlâ** lower house; **majles-e pâ'in** upper house
majruh wound; **majruh kar-dan** to wound
mâkâroni pasta
malâfe sheet; **malâfe-ye tamiz** clean sheets
malakh grasshopper
malaryâ malaria
malek king
mâliyât-e forudgâh airport tax
man I; me
mânde stale
manteghe district *in province*; **manteghe-ye san'ati** industrial estate; **mantaghe-ye min** mine-field
mântô coat
manzare view
mâr snake; **mâr-e kôbrâ** cobra
marâsem-e dafn funeral
maraz-e ghalbi heart condi-tion
mard man; male; person
mardom people

mardomak-e chesm *eye* pupil
marg death
marghzâr meadow
mariz sick
marizi disease; **marizi-ye parvâz** airsickness
markaz center; **markaz-e shahr** city center/town center; **markaz-e telefôn/mokhâberât** telephone center
mârmulak gecko
Mârs March
marz border
mas'ul-e omur-e edâri administrator
masâne bladder
mâse sand
mashgh homework
mâshin car; machine; **mâshin hesâb** calculator; **mâshin-e khayâti** sewing machine; **mâshin-tahrir** typewriter
mashrub alcohol
mashrutiyat constitution
Masihi Christian
masjed mosque
mâst yogurt
matik lipstick
mavâd-e mokhadar drug *narcotic*
mavzu' subject
maydân square; **maydân-e asli** main square
mâye' liquid; **mâye'-ye shostan-e lenz** contact lens solution; **mâye'-ye shostoshu-ye dehan** mouthwash
mâyl mile
maymun monkey
mâzhik felt-tip pen
mazra'e farm; field

meh fog; mist
mehmân-e sokhanrân guest speaker
mehmâni party
Mehr *name of the 7th Iranian month*
mekânik mechanic
meliyat nationality; nation
me'mâr architect
menhâ kardan to subtract
menhâ subtraction
menyu menu
mersi! thank you!
mes copper
meshki black
mesvâk toothbrush
metr meter
metro subway/metro
Mey May
mikh nail
mikrôb-hâ germs
mikroskop microscope
mile-ye barghgir lightning bolt
milyôn million
min *noun* mine; **min-hâ** mines; **min yâb** mine detector; **minbardâri** mine disposal
mish ewe
mive fruit
miyânjigar-e mozâkerât negotiator
miz table; desk; **miz-e chek-in** check-in counter
mo'adab polite
mo'alem teacher
mo'asesa-ye khayriye charity *organization*
moch-e dast wrist
môdem modem
modern modern
mofaser analyst
mohandes engineer

mohâsebe calculation
mohâsere siege
mohemât ammunition; munitions; **mohemât-e monfajer nashode** unexploded ammunition/ordnance
mojarad single
mojasame statue
mokhâberât telecommunications
mokhâlef opponent
mokhâlefat *noun* protest
mokhâlefin opposition
molâghât meeting; **molâghat kardan** to meet
monfajer shodan explosion; to explode
monshi secretary
morabâ jam; jelly
morâje'ât inquiries
mordâb marsh; swamp
Mordâd *name of the 5th Iranian month*
mordan to die
morde dead
morgh chicken; hen; **morgh-e hendi** turkey; **morghân** chickens; **morghân-e khânegi** poultry
morghâbi duck
mosâbeghe match; competition; **mosâbeghe-ye asb** horse racing; **mosâbeghe-ye futbol** soccer match
mosaken painkiller; tranquilizer
Mosalmân Muslim
mosalsal machine gun; **mosalsal-e khodkâr** submachine gun
moshâhede konande observer
moshâver consultant

moshkeli nist! No problem!
mosht fist
mosibat disaster; **mosibat-e tabi'i** natural disaster
mostaghel independent
mostaghim straight on
mota'ahel married *male*
motakâ cushion *large*
motakhases specialist; consultant; **motakhases-e eghtesâd** economist
motarjem translator
motashakeram! thank you
motavaghef kardan to stop
motôr engine; motorbike
movafaghiyat success
moz banana(s)
mozhgân eyelashes
mu hair
murche ant(s)
muryâne termite
mush mouse; **mush-e sahrâ'i** rat
mushak missile; rocket
musigh(i) music; **musighi-ye kelâsik** classical music; **musighi-ye mahali** folk music; **musighi-ye pâp** pop music
muze museum

N

na no; not
nabsh corner
nâdorost false
nâf navel; umbilicus
nafarbar armored car
naghâsh artist
naghshe map; **naghshe-ye râh** road map; **naghshe-ye shahr** city map; **naghshe-ye Tehrân** a map of Tehran

nahâr

nâhâr lunch
nah no
najâr carpenter
najâr joiner
nâkâmi failure
nakh string; thread
nakhâ' spinal column; spine
nakhayr no
nakhi cotton
nâkhon nail *of finger/toe*
nâkhongir nail-clippers
nâkhoshi-ye hamehgir epidemic
nâkhost vazir prime minister
na'l kardan to shoe *a horse*
na'lbaki saucer
nâm name; **nâm-e khânde-vâdegi** surname
namâyeshgâh exhibition
nâme letter
named carpet *felt*
nân bread; **nân-e sândvich** loaf
na'nâ mint
nânvâ'i bakery
nâpokhte uncooked
nârâhat unhappy; uncomfortable
nardebân ladder
nârenjak grenade; shell
nârenji orange
narm soft; tender
navad ninety
navâr cassette; tape; **navâr vidyô** videotape player/recorder
nave granddaughter/grandson
nazdik near; close
ne not
nesf one-half
neshâni sign
neshastan to sit

neveshtan to write
nevisande writer
nezâmi: -(y)e nezâmi military *adjective*
nim-e shab midnight
nimkat bench
nirugâh-e âtomi nuclear power station
niru: niru-ye havâ'i airforce; **niru-ye komaki** reinforcements; **niru-ye âtomi** nuclear energy
nish sting; bite; **nish-e mâr** snakebite
nô new; **Nô Ruz** New Year
noghre silver
noh nine
nôhom ninth
nôjavân teenager
nôk peak; summit
nokhod chickpeas; **nokhod sabz** peas
noskhe copy
Novambr November
nur light
nushidani drink
nuzdah nineteen

O/O

o and
ô he/she/it
oftâdan to fall
ofunat; ofuniyat infection; **Ofuniyat karde.** It is infected.
oghâb eagle
Oktôbr October
operâtor operator; **operâtor-e baynolmelali** international operator
Ordibehesht name of the 2nd Iranian month
ordu-ye asirân-e jangi prisoner-of-war camp

Ortodoks Orthodox
ostâd academic
ostokhun bone; **ostokhun-e rân** femur; **ostokhun-e shâne** shoulder-blade
Ostrâlyâ Australia
Ostrâlyâ'i Australian
otâgh room; **otâgh-e kânfarâns** conference room; **otâgh-e amaliyât** operating theatre/room
Ozbek Uzbek
Ozbekistân Uzbekistan
ozv organ *of body*

P

pâ foot; leg; **pâ-hâ** feet; legs; **pâ-ye masnu'i** artifical leg
pahn wide
pâ'in down; low
pâ'iz autumn; fall
pâk kardan to clear
pâkat envelope
Pâkestân Pakistan
Pâkestâni Pakistani
pâk-kon eraser
palang leopard
palâster Band-Aid; plaster
pâlto coat
pâmp pump
panâh bordan to take shelter
panâhande refugee; **panâhandegân** refugees
panâhgâh shelter
panbe cotton wool
panir cheese
panj five
panjâh fifty
panjere window
panjom fifth
Panjshambe Thursday

pânsyôn guesthouse
pânzdah fifteen
parande bird; **parande-gân** birds
parashut parachute
parastâr nurse
pârch jug
pârche cloth; fabric
parde curtain
pariruz the day before yesterday
pârk park
pârking car park
pârsâl last year
partizan guerrilla
parvande file *paper/computer*
parvâne butterfly
parvâz flight; **parvâz-e baynolmelali** international flight; **parvâz-e dâkheli** national/ internal flight
pas-e after
pasfardâ the day after tomorrow
pashe(-hâ) mosquito(es)
pashekhâne mosquito net
pashm wool
pâshne heel
pâspôrt passport
patu blanket
pedar father; **pedar bozorg** grandfather
pelâstik plastic
pele stairs; **pele barghi** escalator
pesar son; **pesar bache** baby boy
peshak-e vahshi mongoose
pestân breasts/bust
peste pistachio
pezeshk-e motakhases-e bihushi anesthetist

pich screw
pichkoshti screwdriver
pir old
pirâhan dress; shirt
piruzi victory
pish-e ruye in front of
pishraft progress
pitsa pizza
piyâde on foot
piyârsâl the year before last
piyâz onion/onions
plâg (bath) plug
pokhte cooked
pol bridge
polav *rice: cooked*
polis police; **polis-e seri** secret police
pond(-e esterling) pound (sterling)
por full; **por-e sarsedâ** noisy
Portagâli Portuguese
portoghâl orange
posht back; behind
post post; **post-e havâ'i** air mail; **post-e sefâreshi** registered mail
postkhâne post office
printer printer
prozhektar projector
pudr powder; **pudr-e lebâs shu'i** washing powder; detergent
pul money; currency; **pul-e khord** loose change
pust skin
putinhâ rubber boots

R

rad veto; **rad kardan** to veto
ra'd thunder; **ra'd o bargh** thunderstorm
râdyâtor radiator
radyô radio

raftan to go
rag artery; vein
ragbâr shower *of rain*
râgbi rugby
raghs dancing; **raghs-e mahali** folk dancing
râh path; way; road; **râh âhan** railway; **râh-e 'obur** footpath; **Râh dârid barâye ma'alulin?** Do you have access for the disabled?
rahâ kardan to liberate
râhat comfortable
râhbandân roadblock
rahbar leader
rahem womb
râhnamâ indicator light
ra'is leader; chairman/chairwoman; **ra'is jomhur** president; **ra'is-e setâd** chief of staff
râket rocket
Ramazân Ramadan
rân thigh
rânande driver
rang color; paint
rangin kamân rainbow
râst right; **Râst migid.** You are right.
rasturân restaurant
râsu ferret
ravâbet-e diplômâtik diplomatic ties
ra'y vote; **ra'y dâdan** voting; **ra'y-e aghaliyat** minority vote
raziyâne fennel
resâne-hâ the media
resid receipt
reside ripe
rezerv shode reserved
rezhim diet
rimel mascara

rishe beard; root; **rish-safid** elder (of village, etc.)

rishtarâsh (barghi) (electric) razor

riyâzi maths

rizhehgar-e olum-e siyâsi political analyst

rob' one-quarter; district *in town*

rôghan oil; ghee; oinment

român novel; **român-hâ be zabân-e Ingilisi** a novel in English

roshd kardan to grow

ru cheek; front; on; **ru-be-ru** opposite

rubâh fox

rubel ruble

rud stream

rude gut; **rude-hâ** intestines

rudel indigestion

rudkhâne river

rumizi tablecloth *table*

Rus Russia

rusari headscarf

Rusi Russian

ruz day; daytime; **ruz be khayr!** good afternoon!

ruznâme newspaper; **ruz-nâme be zabân-e Ingilisi** newspaper in English

S/SH

sâ'at hour; o'clock; watch; clock; **sâ'at sâz** watchmaker's

sabad basket

sabok light

sâbun soap

sabz green

sabzi: sabzi forush greengrocer; **sabzi forushi** vegetable shop

sabzijât vegetables

sad hundred; dam

sade century

safar journey; **safar be khayr!** bon voyage!

safe record

safhe page

safir ambassador

sag dog; **sag-e gale** sheepdog; **sag-e mâhi** sturgeon

sâgh-e pâ calf *of leg*

saghf ceiling

sahrâ desert

sâk bag; carrier bag

sâket quiet

sakht difficult

sâkhtemân building; **sâkhtemân-e âpârtemân** apartment block/building

sakn podium

sakte: sakte-ye ghalbi heart attack; **sakte-ye maghzi** *medical* stroke

saku platform; **saku-ye partâb-e mushak** rocket-launcher

sâl year

sâlâd salad

salâm! hello!

salâmat(i) health; **salâmat bâshid!** health to you!

sâl-e âyande next year

sâlem well

Salib-e Sorkh Red Cross

salmâni barber; hairdresser

sâlon-e kânsert concert hall

san'at industry

sanâ'ye industry; **sanâ'ye-ye hoteldâri** hotel industry; **sanâ'ye-ye jehângardi** tourism; **sanâ'ye dasti** handicraft

sandal(-ha) sandal(s)

sandali chair; seat; **sandali-ye charkhdâr** wheelchair

sandogh chest; **sandogh-e aghab** boot/trunk *of car*; **sandogh posti** mailbox

sandughdâr cashier

sândvich sandwich

sang posht tortoise; turtle

sang stone; rock

sangin heavy

sâniye *noun* second

sanjâb squirrel

sanjâghok dragonfly

sanjâgh pin; **sanjâgh ghofli** safety pin

sar head; **sar lashkar** *military* general

sarâfi bureau de change

sarbân captain

sarbâz soldier; **sarbâzân** troops; **sarbâz-e mozdur** mercenary

sarchesme spring of water

sard cold

saretân cancer

sarhang dovum lieutenant-colonel

sari' quick; **sari'-us-sayr** express

sarlashkar major-general

sarmâ khordegi cold *medical*

sarnize bayonet

sartip lieutenant-general

satl bucket

savâri passenger

sayâhat tourism

sayâre planet

sayl flood

saylâb torrent

Sazemân-e Anjoman-e Helâl-e Ahmar-e Irân Iranian Red Crescent

Sâzemân-e Melal-e Motahed United Nations

sebil mustache

sedâ noise

sefârat embassy

sefid white

sefr zero

seft hard; tough

seh three; **seh rob'** three-quarters; **seh ruz pish** three days before

sehbâr three times

seh-shâkhe *three-pin electric* plug

Sehshambe Tuesday

seke coins

sel tuberculosis

selsele-ye kuhi mountain range

sen age

senf: senf-e khorda forushi retail industry; **senf-e tafrihâti** leisure industry

senjâgh-e sine brooch

separ bumper

Septambr September

serke vinegar

seshuâr hairdryer

setâd personnel; **setâd-e artesh** *military* staff

setâre star; **setâre-gân** stars

sevom third

shab night; **shab be khayr!** good night!

shabnam dew

shafâ khâne dispensary

shâgerd pupil

shaghal jackal

shahid martyr

shâhin falcon

shahr town; city; **shahr-e ghadim(i)** old city

shahrak housing estate/project

Shahrivar *name of the 6th Iranian month*

shakhsi personal

shâl shawl
shalil nectarine
shâlgardan scarf
shalgham turnip
shalvâr trousers
shâm dinner; supper
sham' candle; **sham'-hâ** candles; **sham'-dân** candlestick
Shambe Saturday
shâmel: shâmel shode included; **shâmel na-shode** excluded
shâmpu shampoo
shâne shoulder; comb
shânzdah sixteen
sharâb wine
sharbat syrup; **sharbat-e limu** lemon squash
shargh east
shast sixty; thumb
shatranj chess
shôhar husband
shehâdat dâdan to testify
shekam stomach
shekanje torture
shekar sugar
shekast defeat; **shekast dâdan** to beat; to defeat
shekastagi fracture
shelik nakonid! don't shoot!
shen gravel/sand
shenâ swimming
shenidan to hear
shepesh louse; lice
shesh six
sheshom sixth
Shi'a Shi'ism
Shi'a; Ahl-e Shi'a Shi'ite
shilang hose
shir milk; lion; **shir-e boz** goat's milk; **shir-e gâv** cow's milk; **shir-e mâdar** mother's milk; **shir-e pudr** powdered milk
shire treacle
shirin sweet
shishe bottle; glass; windscreen/windshield; **yek shishe âb** a bottle of water; **yek shishe-ye digar** another bottle
shodan to be
shoghl profession
shôhardâr married *female*
shokhm zadan to plow
shomâ you *plural/formal*
shomâl north
shomârdan to count
shomâre number; **shomâre-ye otâgh** room number; **shomâre-ye pâsport** passport number; **shomâre-ye saku** platform number; **shomâre-ye mâshin** car registration
shoru' beginning
shosh lung
shotor camel
shrapnel shrapnel
shur salty
Shurâ-ye Negahbân Council of Guardians
shuru' kardan to start
si thirty
sib apple; **sib zamini** potato/potatoes; **sib zamini sorkh karde** french fries
si-di C.D.
sigâr keshidan mamnu' ast no smoking
sim wire; **sim-e boksol** tow rope; **sim-e khârdâr** barbed wire
sine chest; **sineband** brassiere
sinemâ cinema
sini tray
sir garlic

siyâh black
siyâsat politics
siyâsatmadâr politician
sizdah thirteen
so'âl question
sobh morning; in the morning; **sobh be khayr!** good morning!
sobhâne breakfast
sofre tablecloth *floor*
soghât forushi souvenir shop
sohbat kardan to talk
sokhanrân speaker
sokut silence
solh peace; truce; **solh kardan** to make peace
Sonat Sunnism; **Ahl-e Sonat** Sunni
sonati traditional
Soni Sunni
sôranj syringe
sorfe cough
sôs sauce; ketchup
sôsis sausage
sosyâlist socialist
sosyâlizm socialism
sotvân lieutenant
sukht fuel
sup soup
super supermarket
surâkh-e dokme buttonhole
surat face
surati pink
susk cockroach
susmâr lizard; gecko
suzan needle
suzesh *noun* burn

T

tâ to; up to; until; **tâ fardâ!** see you tomorrow!
tab fever; temperature
tab'id exile

tabaghe floor *story*
tabar ax
tâbe' citizen
tâbe'iyat nationality
tâbestân summer
tabl-e gush ear drum
tafrih a break *for refreshments*
tagarg hail
tâghche shelf
ta'ghib kardan to pursue
taghsim division; **taghsim kardan** to divide
tâh bottom
tâjer trader; business person
Tâjik Tajik
Tâjikistân Tajikistan
takhalof-e ra'y vote-rigging
ta'khir delay
takhliye kardan to evacuate
takht bed; **takht-e dô nafari** double bed
takhte plank; **takhte siyâh** blackboard
tâkhtotâz invasion; **tâkhtotâz kardan** to invade
tâksi telefôni radio taxi
talâ' gold
talâgh shode divorced
tâlâr-e operâ opera house
tâlebi cantelope melon
talkh bitter
tamâm kardan to finish
tambali laziness
tambr stamp
tamiz clean
tanâb rope
tanbih kardan to punish
tane trunk *of tree*
tânk tank
tapânche gun; pistol

tut

tape hill
taraf side of body
tarâh designer
târik dark
târikh date; history; **târikh-e tavalod** date of birth; **târikh-e khoruj** date of departure; **târikh-e vorud** date of arrival
târiki darkness
tarjome translation
tarkesh shrapnel
tasbih rosary
tasdigh-e rânandegi driver's license
tashakor! thank you!
tashrif beyârid! come again!
taslim kardan to surrender
tasne-ye parvâne fan belt
ta'tilât holidays
tavalod birth
tavânestan to be able
tâvus peacock
tayâre-ye jangi bomber plane
tâze fresh
te'âtr theatre
tejârat business
tekrâr kardan to repeat
telefôn telephone; **telefôn-e dasti** mobile phone/ cell phone; **telefôn-e mâhvâre** satellite phone
telefônchi switchboard operator
teleskop telescope
televizyon television; **tele-vizyon-e dasti** portable T.V.
terâktôr tractor
terâpist therapist
terâs veranda

terâvelchek-hâ traveler's checks
terayli truck/lorry; trailer
teror assassination
teshne thirsty; **Man teshne hastam.** I'm thirsty.
tigh razor blade
tim team
Tir name of the 4th Iranian month
tirmâr viper
tô you singular
tofang gun; rifle
tokhm/tokhom egg; seeds; **tokhm-e âb paz** boiled egg
tôl-baks tool box
tolu' sunrise
ton ton; tonne
tond quick; spicy; hot
Tork Turkish
Torkaman Turkmen
Torkamanestân Turkmen-istan
Torkiye Turkey
tormoz brake
torobche radish
torsh sour
toshak mattress
tôzi' distribution
tôzih dâdan to explain
trânsformer transformer
tu inside
tufân storm; **tufân-e tagarg** hailstorm
tunel tunnel; **tunel-e zir zamin** metro/subway
tup ball; cannon
tupkhâne artillery
turist tourist
turizm tourism
tut mulberry; **tut farangi** strawberries

tuti

tuti parrot
tuvâlet toilet; **tuvâlet-e zanâne tuvâlet-e mardâne** ladies/gents toilets

U

Urupâ Europe
Ut August
utu iron *for clothing*

V

va and
vâ'isin! stop!
vaght time
vâgon-e takhtkhâbdâr sleeping car *of train*
vakil lawyer
vali but
vânet van
varaghe sheet *of paper*
varam edema
vârni; vârnish varnish
varzesh exercise
vasâ'el-e nezâmi artillery
vasl kardan to transfer/put through
Vaylz Wales
vaz' haml birth; childbirth
vaze' ezterâri emergency
vazir minister
vaz'iyat-e ezdevâji marital status
vezârat ministry; **Vezârat-e Âmuzesh va Parvaresh** Ministry of Education; **Vezârat-e Behdâsht** Ministry of Health; **Vezârat-e Dâdgostari** Ministry of Justice; **Vezârat-e Defâ'** Ministry of Defense; **Vezârat-e Etelâ'ât** Ministry of Information; **Vezârat-e Farhang** Ministry of Culture; **Vezârat-e Keshâvarzi** Ministry of Agriculture; **Vezârat-e Keshvar** Ministry of Home Affairs; **Vezârat-e Eghtesâd** Ministry of Finance; **Vezârat-e Omur-e Khâreji** Ministry of Foreign Affairs; **Vezârat-e Tejârat ve Sanâye** Ministry of Commerce and Industry; **Vezârat-e Turizm** Ministry of Tourism
vitâmin-hâ vitamins
viza visa
vorud arrivals; **vorud mamnu' (ast)** no entry
vorud entrance

Y

yâ or
yâd: yâd dâdan to teach; **yâd gereftan** to learn
Yahudi Jewish
yakh ice; **yakhchâl** fridge; ice-box; **yakhshekan** ice ax; ice pick; **yakh zadagi** frostbite; **yakh bandân** frost; **yakh bastan** to freeze
yaghe collar
yârd *measurement* yard
yatim orphan
yavâsh slow; **yavâsh!** gently!
yâzdah eleven
-ye/-e of
yek one; a/an; **yek sevom** one-third
yekbâr once
Yekshambe Sunday
yobs constipation; **yobs hastid?** are you constipated?

yuro euro

Z/ZH
zabân language
zabân tongue
zabt: zabt kardan to record; **mâshin zabt** tape recorder
zadan to hit
zâ'idan to give birth to
za'if weak
zamân-e hâzer present
zamin earth; land; **zamin-e futbol** pitch; **zamin-e bâyer** fallowland
zan woman; wife; female; **zanân** women
zanbur bee; wasp; **zanbur-e sorkh** hornet
zang rust
zanjir chain
zânu knee
zarb multiplication; **zarb kardan** to multiply
zard yellow
zardâlu apricot
zaytun olives
zed-e anti-; **zed-e ofuni** anti-

septic; **zed-e yakh** anti-freeze
Zeland-e Naw New Zealand
zelzele earthquake
zemestân winter
zendân prison
zende alive; **zende budan** to be alive
zendegi life
zenjebil ginger
zhâkat jacket
Zhânviye January
Zhâpân Japan
Zhâpâni Japanese
Zhu'an June
Zhu'iye July
zip zipper
zir under; **zir-e kafsh** sole of shoe; **zir sigâri** ashtray; **zir zamin** metro/subway
zirpush underwear; under-shirt/vest
ziyâd many; too; too much/many
ziyâratgâh shrine
zohr noon
zomord-e sabz emerald
zorat maize

ENGLISH—FARSI
INGILISI—FARSI

A

able: to be able tavânestan
academic *person* ostâd
academy akâdemi
accelerator gâz
access: Do you have access for the disabled? Râh dârid barâye ma'alulin?
accommodation eghâmat-gâh
accountant hesâbdâr
acre ayker
adapter âdâptôr
add jam' kardan
addition jam'
address âdres
administrator mas'ul-e omur-e edâri
advertising e'lânât
Afghani Afghâni
Afghanistan Afghânestân
after pas-e
afternoon ba'd az zohr; **good afternoon!** roz be khayr!; **in the afternoon** ba'd az zohr; **this afternoon** emruz ba'd az zohr
age sen
agenda âzhendâ
agriculture keshâvarzi
agronomist keshâvarzi shenâs
aid komak; **aid agency** âzhâns-e emdâd; **aid worker** madâdkâr; kâr-gar-e emdâdi
AIDS aydz

air havâ; **air mail** post-e havâ'i
airdrop ghuyud
airforce niru-ye havâ'i
airplane havâpaymâ
airport forudgâh; **airport tax** mâliyât-e forudgâh
air-raid hamle-ye havâ'i
airsickness marizi-ye parvâz
alcohol mashrub
alcoholism e'tiyâdi be alkol
alive zende
all hame; **that's all!** Bas e!; Hamin!
allergic: I'm allergic to penicillin. Be penisilin hasâsiyat dâram.
allergy hasâsiyat
almond bâdâm
also ham
altitude sickness bimâri-ye ertefâ
ambassador safir
amber kahrabâ
ambulance âmbulâns
ambush kamin
America Âmrikâ
American Âmrikâ'i
ammunition mohemât
amputate ghat'-e andâm kardan
analyst mofaser
ancient ghadimi
and ve; o
anemia kam khuni
anesthetic davâ-ye bihushi
anesthetist pezeshk-e mota-

khases-e bihushi
animal hayvân; **animals**
hayvânât
ankle ghuzak
another -e digar; **another**
bottle yek shishe-ye digar
answer javâb
ant(s) murche
antelope gavazn
anti-aircraft gun aslahe-ye
zed-e havâ'i
antibiotic ântibiyotik
anti-freeze zed-e yakh
antiseptic zed-e ofuni
apartment âpârtemân
apartment block/building
sâkhtemân-e âpârtemân
appetite eshtehâ
apple sib
apricot zardâlu
April Âvril
Aquarius Dalv
Arab Arab
archeological bâstâni
architect me'mâr
Aries Hamal
arm dast
Armenia Armanestân
Armenian Armani
armored car nafarbar
arms aslahe
army artesh
arrest dastgir kardan
arrive residan
arrivals vorud
art gallery gâleri(-ye honari)
artery rag
article maghâle
artifical -e masnu'i; **artifical**
arm dast-e mashu'i;
artifical leg pâ-ye masnu'i; **artifical eye**
cheshm-e masnu'i

artillery tupkhâne; vasâ'el-e
nezâmi
artist naghâsh
ashtray zir sigâri
aspirin âspirin
assassination teror
assault; attack hamle
assembly *meeting* anjoman
at dar; be; **at the traffic**
lights dam-e cheragh
ghermez
aubergine bâdemjân
August Ut
Australia Ostrâlyâ
Australian Ostrâlyâ'i
autonomy khod mokhtâri
autumn; fall pâ'iz
avalanche bahman
aviation havânavardi
ax tabar
axle aksal
ayatollah âyatolâh
Azerbaijan Âzarbâyjân
Azerbaijani Âzarbâyjâni

B
baby bache; **baby girl**
dokhtar bache; **baby boy**
pesar bache
back posht
backache kamar dard
backpack kul-e poshti
backwardss aghab
bad bad; *spoiled* kharâb
badly kharâb
bag kif; sâk
baggage bâr; **baggage**
counter ghesmat-e bâr
baker's nânvâ'i
bakery nânvâ'i
balcony balkon
ball tup
ballpoint pen khodkâr

Baluchi

Baluchi Baluch
banana(s) moz
bandage bând
bandaid *plaster* chasp
Band-Aid; plaster palaster
bangle alangu
bank bânk; **bank notes** eskenâs-e bânki
banker bânkdâr
bar bâr
barbed wire sim-e khârdâr
barber's shop salmâni
barley jô
barn kahdân
barren *land* bihâsel; khoshk
basket sabad
basketball bâsketbâl
bat *animal* khofâsh
bathroom hamâm
battery bâtri
bayonet sarnize
bazaar bazâr
be budan; shodan
beans lubiyâ
bear khers
beard rishe
beat *to overcome* shekast dâdan
bed takht
bee zanbur
beef gusht-e gâv
beer âb-e jô
beetroot choghondar
beginning shoru'
behind posht
belt kamarband
bench nimkat
better behtar
bicycle dô-charkhe
big bozorg
bill hesâb
binoculars durbin
bird parande; **birds** parande-gân

biro khodkâr
birth tavalod; **childbirth** vaz' haml; **to give birth to** zâ'idan
bit: a little bit yek (meghdâr-e) kam
bite nish
bitter talkh
black siyâh; meshki; **black and white film** film-se siyâh o sefid
blackboard takhte siyâh
blacksmith âhangar
bladder masâne
blanket patu
blizzard bâd-e shadid bâ barf
blood khun; **blood group** grup-e khun; **blood pressure** feshâr-e khun; **blood transfusion** enteghâl-e khun
blue âbi
boar gorâz
boarding pass kârt-e savâr shodan
boat ghâyegh
body badan
boiled egg tokhm-e morgh-e âb paz
bomb bômb
bomb bombarân kardan
bomber plane tayâre-ye jangi
bon voyage! safar be khayr!
bone ostokhun
bonnet kâput
book ketâb
bookshop/bookstore ketâb-forushi
boot chakme; *of car* san-dogh-e aghab; **boots** chakmehâ
boots: rubber boots putinhâ

border marz
born: to be born motavaled shodan; **Where were you born?** Shomâ kojâ be donyâ âmadid?; **I was born in ...** Man dar ... be donyâ âmadam.
bottle shishe; **bottle of water** shishe âb
bottle-opener dar bâz-kon
bottom bâsan; tâh
bowl kâse
box ja'be
boy pesar
bra; brassiere sineband
bracelet dastband
brain maghz
brake tormoz
brandy konyâk
bread nân
break *for refreshments* tafrih
breakfast sobhâne
brick âjor
bridge pol
Britain Baritânyâ; Ingilis
British Ingilisi
brooch senjâgh-e sina
brother barâdar
brown ghahve'i
brush boros
brush ghalam-e mu
bucket satl
Buddhist az maz-hab-e Budâ
buffalo bufâlô
bug *insect* jânevar
building sâkhtemân
bull gâv-e nar
bullet golule
bumper separ
bureau de change sarâfi
burger berger
burn *noun* suzesh
bus otobus
bus stop/bus station istgâh-

e otobus
business tejârat; **business person** kâseb; tâjer
bust pestân
but amâ; vali
butcher's shop ghasâbi
butt *of rifle* kune-ye tofang
butter kare
butterfly parvâne
button dokme
buttonhole surâkh-e dokme

C

cabbage kalam
cabinet kâbine
cable kâbl
café ghahvekhâne; kâfi
cake kayki shirini
calculation mohâsebe
calculator mâshin hesâb
calf gusâle
calf *of leg* sâgh-e pâ
camel shotor
camera durbin; **camera equipment** lavâzem-e film-vardâri
camouflage estefâr kardan
campsite jâ-ye châdor zadan
can ghuti; **can opener** dar-bâz kon
Canada Kânâdâ
Canadian Kânâdâ'i
canal kânâl
cancer; Cancer saretân
candle sham'; **candles** sham'-hâ
candlestick sham'-dân
candy âb nabât
cannon tup
cantelope *melon* tâlebi
Capricorn Jadi
captain sarbân
car mâshin; **car park** pârk-

ing; **car papers** madâreke mâshin; **car registration** shomâre-ye mâshin
carpenter najâr
carpet *felt* named; *knotted* farsh; *woven* gelim
carpet: *rug* ghâli; ghâliche
carriage *horse-drawn* gâri
carrier bag sâk
carrots havich
carry haml kardan
cartridge *for gun* fishang
cashier sandughdâr
cassette navâr
castle ghal'e
cat gorbe
caterpillar kerm-e sad-pâ
Catholic Kâtulik
cattle gale-ye gâv
cauliflower gol kalam
cave ghâr
caviar khâvyâr
courtesy adab
C.D. si-di; **C.D. player** dastgâh-e si-di
ceasefire âteshbas
ceiling saghf
cell phone telefôn-e dasti
cemetery ghabrestân
center markaz
century sade; gharn
chador châdor
chain zanjir
chair sandali
chairman/chairwoman ra'is
chalk gach
change: loose change pul-e khord
charity *organization* mo'asesa-ye khayriye
cheap arzân
check-in chek-in; **check-in counter** miz-e chek-in
checkpoint istgâh-e bâzrasi-ye marz
cheek ru; gune
cheese panir
chemist's *pharmacy* dârukhâne
cherry gilâs
chess shatranj
chest *of body* sine; *box* sandogh
chewing gum âdâms
chicken morgh
chickpeas nokhod
chief of staff ra'is-e setâd
child bache; **children** bache-hâ
chin châne
China Chin
Chinese Chini
choke khafe shoden; **He/She is choking!** Khafe mishavad!
cholera kolerâ
choose entekhâb kardan
Christian Masihi
church kelisâ
cinema sinemâ
circumcision khatne
citizen tâbe'
city shahr; **city center** markaz-e shahr; **city map** naghshe-ye shahr
civil: civil rights hoghugh-e madani; **civil servant** kârmand-e dôlat; **civil war** jang-e dâkheli
class kelâs
classical music musigh-e kelâsik
clean tamiz; **clean sheets** malâfe-ye tamiz
clear *verb* pâk kardan
climate âb o havâ
clinic klinik
clock sâ'at

closed baste
cloth pârche
clothes lebâs; **clothes shop** lebâs-forushi
cloud abr
cloudy abri
cluster bomb bômb-e khoshe'i
clutch kalâch
coat pâlto; mântô
cobra mâr-e kôbrâ
cockroach susk
coffee ghahve; **coffee with milk** ghahve bâ shir
coins seke
cold sard; *medical* sarmâ khordegi; **cold water** âb-e sard
collar yaghe
colleague hamkâr
college kâlej
color rang; **color film** film-e rangi
comb shâne
combine harvester kambâyn
come âmadan; **come again!** tashrif beyârid!; **come in!** befârma'id!; **come to the table!** befarmâ'id!
comfortable râhat
command farmân dâdan
commission komisyun
communications ertebât
communism komunizm
communist komunist
companion: traveling companion hamsafar
compass ghotbnamâ
computer kâmpyuter
concert kânsert; **concert hall** sâlon-e kânsert
condemn mahkum kardan
condom kâput

conference kânfarâns; **conference room** otâgh-e kânfarâns
conquer ghâleb shodan (bar)
constipated: are you constipated? yobs hastid?
constipation yobs
constitution mashrutiyat
consulate konsulgari
consultant moshâver; motakhases
contact lenses lenz; **contact lens solution** mâye'-ye shostan-e lenz
convoy kârvân
cook âshpazi kardan
cooked pokhte
cooker gâz; *(hob)* cherâgh
cool sard; khonak
copper mes
copy *noun* noskhe; *verb* kâpi kardan
coriander gishniz
corkscrew dar bâz-kon
corn ghale
corner gushe; nabsh
corruption fesâd
cotton nakhi; **cotton wool** panbe
cough sorfe
council shurâ; **Council of Guardians** Shurâ-ye Negahbân
count shomârdan
coup d'etat kudetâ
cow gâv
co-wife havu
crab kharchang
crayon madâd sham'i
cream *ointment* krem
credit card kârt-e e'tebâr
cricket *insect* jirjirak; *game* kriket

crime jorm; jenâyat
criminal jenâyatkâr
crisis bohrân
crops mahsul
crossroads chahâr-râh
crow kalâgh
crowbar ahram
crutch chub dasti
crystal kristâl; bolur
cucumber khiyâr
cultivate kesht kardan
cup fenjân
cupboard ghafase
currency pul
curtain parde
cushion *large* motakâ; *small* kusan
customs gomrok
cut *verb* boridan

D

dagger khanjar
dairy labaniyât
dam sad
dancing raghs
danger khatar; danger! Khatar!
dark târik
darkness târiki
date târikh; *fruit* khormâ; date of birth târikh-e tavalod; date of arrival târikh-e vorud; date of departure târikh-e khoruj
daughter dokhtar
dawn fajr
day ruz; the day before yesterday pariruz; the day after tomorrow pasfardâ
daytime ruz
dead morde
death marg

debt bedehkâri; gharz
decade dôre-ye dah sâleh
December Desambr
deer âhu; gavazn
defeat shekast kardan
defeat: *noun* shekast
dehydration kam âbi
delay ta'khir
democracy demôkrâsi
dentist dandân pezeshk; dandân-sâz; dentist's surgery dandân-forush
deodorant atr
department store forushgâh
departures khoruj
desert sahrâ
designer tarâh
desk miz
dessert deser
destroy kharâb kardan
detergent pudr-e lebâs shu'i
detonation monfajer shodan
dew shabnam
diarrhea es-hâl
dictator diktâtôr
dictatorship diktâtôri
dictionary farhang
die mordan
diet rezhim
difficult sakht
digital dijitâl
dining car *of train* bufe
dinner shâm
diplomat diplumât
diplomatic -e diplômâtik; diplomatic ties ravâbet-e diplômâtik
dirty kasif
disabled person ma'alul; disabled people ma'alulin
disaster mosibat
disco diskô
discussion bahs

disease marizi
dispensary shafâ khâne
displaced person âdam-e tab'idi; displaced persons âdam-hâ-ye tab'idi
distribution tôzi'
district *in province* mantaghe; *in town* rob'
divide taghsim kardan
division taghsim
divorced talâgh shode
doctor doktur-e pezeshk
dog sag
dollar dolâr
donkey khar
door dâr
doorlock ghofl-e dâr
double -e dô; double bed takht-e dô nafari
dove kabutar
down pâ'in
dragonfly sanjâghok
drawer keshô
dress lebâs; pirâhan
dressing *medical* bândâzh
dressmaker khayât
drill *tool* deril
drink *verb* khordan; *noun* nushidani
drinking water âb khordan
drive *verb* rânandegi kardan; *noun* neutral drive dande-ye khalâs
driver rânande
driver's license tasdigh-e rânandegi
drought khoshk sâli
drug *medical* davâ; dâru; *narcotic* mavâd-e mokhadar
duck morghâbi
Dutch Holândi
D.V.D. di-vi-di; D.V.D.

player dastgâh-e di-vi-di
dysentery es-hâl khuni

E

eagle oghâb
ear gush; ears gush-hâ; ear drum tabl-e gush
earrings gushvâre
earth *land* zamin
earthquake zelzele
east shargh
easy âsân
eat khordan
economist motakhases-e eghtesâd
edema varam
egg tokhom
eight hasht
eighteen hijdah
eighth hashtom
eighty hashtâd
elbow ârenj
elder *of village, etc.* rish-safid
election(s) entekhâbât
electric razor rishtarâsh barghi
electrical goods store forushgâh-e lavâzem-e elektriki
electricity bargh
elephant fil
elevator âsânsur
eleven yâzdah
e-mail imayl
embassy sefârat
emerald zomord-e sabz
emergency vaze' ezterâri; emergency exit khoruj-e ezterâri
empty khâli
end âkhar
enemy doshman
engine motôr

engineer mohandes

England Ingilis

English Inglisi

enough bas; kâfi; **that's enough** bas ast

entrance vorud

entry vorud; **no entry** vorud mamnu' (ast)

envelope pâkat

epidemic nâkhoshi-ye hamehgir

eraser pâk-kon

escalator pele barghi

ethnic cleansing koshtar-e nezhâdi

ethnic minority aghaliyat-e nezhâdi

euro yuro

Europe Urupâ

evacuate takhliye kardan

evening asr; ghorub; **good evening!** shab tân khosh!; **in the evening** asr; **this evening** emruz asri

ewe mish

exam emtehân

excess ezâfe; **baggage** bâr-e ezâfe

exchange arz

excluded shâmel nashode

excuse me! bebakhshid!

exercise varzesh

exercise book daftarche

exhaust ekzâst

exhibition namâyeshgâh

exile tab'id

exit khoruj

expensive gerân

explain tôzih dâdan

explode monfajer shodan

express sari'-us-sayr

extension number shomâre-ye dâkheli

extra ezâfe; **an extra blanket** yek patu-ye ezâfe

eye cheshm; **eyes** cheshm-hâ; **eyebrow** abru; **eyelashes** mozhgân; **eyesight** binâyi

F

fabric pârche

face surat

facilities emkânât; **Do you have facilities for the disabled?** Emkânât dârid barâye ma'alulin?

factory worker kârgar

faculty fâkulti

failure nâkâmi

falcon shâhin

fall oftâdan

fallowland zamin-e bâyer

false nâdorost

family khânavâde

famine ghahti

fan havâkesh; **fan belt** tasne-ye parvâne

far dur

farm mazra'e

farmer keshâvarz

farming keshâvarzi

fat charbi

father pedar

fax fâks; **fax machine** dastgâh-e fâks

February Fevriye

feed *an animal* khorâk dâdan

feeding station markaz-e âzughe

feet pâ-hâ

felt-tip pen mâzhik

female zan

femur ostokhun-e rân

fennel raziyâne

ferret râsu

ferry keshti
fertile hâselkhiz
fertilizer kud
fever tab
field mazra'e
fifteen pânzdah
fifth panjom
fifty panjâh
fig anjir
fighter *soldier* jangande
file *paper/computer* parvande
film film
film-maker filmsâz
final *noun* fâynal
fine khob
finger angosht; **fingers** angosht-hâ
finish tamâm kardan
fire âtesh
firefly kerm-e shab tâb
firewood hizom
first aval
fish mâhi
fist mosht
five panj
flash felâsh
flashlight cherâgh ghove
flea kik; kayk
flipflops dampâ'i
flock *of sheep* gale
flood sayl
floor *story* tabaghe
florist gol-forush
flour ârd
flu ânfluyenzâ
fly magas
fog meh
foggy meh-âlud
folk: folk dancing raghs-e mahali; **folk music** musighi-ye mahali
foot pâ; *measurement* fut; **on foot** piyâde

football futbol
foothills dâmane-ye kuh
footpath râh-e 'obur
for barây-e; bare
foreign exchange/currency arz
forest jangal
fork changâl
fort dezh
fortnight dô hafte
forty chehel
forwards jelô
fountain pen ghalam
four chahâr
fourteen chahârdah
fourth chahârom
four-wheel drive jip
fox rubâh
fracture shekastagi
free *adjective* âzâd; *verb* **free** âzâd kardan
freedom âzâdi
freeze yakh bastan
French Farânsavi
french fries sib zamini sorkh karde
fresh tâze
Friday Jom'e; **Friday mosque** masjed-e Jom'e
fridge yakhchâl
friend dust
frog ghurbâghe
from az
front ru; **in front of** jelô
frontier marz
frost yakh bandân; **frostbite** yakh zadagi
fruit mive; **fruit juice** âb mive
fuel sukht
full por; **full moon** ghors-e mâh
funeral marâsem-e dafn
future âyande

gall bladder

G

gall bladder kise-ye sofrâ
gallon gâlôn
garden bâgh
garlic sir
gas gâz; gas canister kâpsul-e gâz
gazelle ghazâl
gear dande
gecko mârmulak
Gemini Jôzâ
general *person* sar lashkar
genitals âlât-e tanâsoli
gently! yavâsh!
geography joghrâfi
Georgia Gorjestân
Georgian Gorjestâni
German Âlemâni
Germany Âlmân
germs mikrôb-hâ
get gereftan
ghee rôghan
gift hediye; kâdô
ginger zenjebil
girl dokhtar
give dâdan
glacier yakh rud
glass livân; gelâs; glass of water yek livân âb
glasses *eyeglasses* aynak
gloves dastkesh
glue chasp
go raftan; go! berid!
goal gol
goat boz; goat meat gusht-e boz
gold talâ'
good khob
goodbye! khodâ hâfez!
goose ghâz
government hokumat
gram grâm
grammar dastur zabân

granddaughter nave
grandfather pedar bozorg
grandmother mâdar bozorg
grandson nave
grape(s) angur
grapefruit gerepfrut
grass chaman
grasshopper malakh
gravel shen
gravy âb-e gusht
green sabz
greengrocer sabzi forush
grenade nârenjak
grey khâkastari
grind âsyâb kardan
grow roshd kardan
guerrilla cherik; partizan
guest speaker mehmân-e sokhanrân
guesthouse pânsyôn
guidebook ketâb-e râhnamâ
gun tofang; *pistol* tapânche; gun barrel boshke-ye mohemât
gut rude

H

hail tagarg
hailstorm tufân-e tagarg
hair mu
hairbrush boros
haircut: I'd like a haircut please. Lotfan muhâm-râ bezanid.
hairdresser salmâni
hairdryer seshuâr
hammer chakosh
hand dast
handbag kif
handicraft sanâye' dasti
handkerchief dastmâl
handle dastgir
handset gushi

happy khosh-hâl

hard seft

hardware store khorde forushi

harvest kharman

hat kolâh

have dâshtan

hawk bâz

hay alaf-e khoshk

he ô; u

head sar

headscarf rusari

health salâmat; **health to you!** salâmat bâshid!

hear shenidan

heart ghalb; **heart attack** sakte-ye ghalbi; **heart condition** maraz-e ghalbi

heater yek bukhâri

heatstroke âftâb zadegi

heatwave garmâ-ye fôgh-ul'âde

heavy sangin

hedgehog khârposht

heel pâshne

helicopter helikoptar

hello! salâm!

help *noun* komak; *verb* komak kardan; **help yourself!** *to food* befarmâ'id!; **help!** komak!; **help me!** man-ô komak konid!

hen morgh

hepatitis hepâtit

herd gale

here injâ; **here is ...** ... injâ-st.; **here are ...** ... injâ-nd.

high boland; **high blood pressure** feshâr-e bâlâ

hill tape

him ô

Hindu Hendu

hip mafsal-e rân

history târikh

hit zadan

H.I.V. ech-ây-vi

holidays ta'tilât

home khâne; **may your home be forever!** khâne âbâd!

homework mashgh

honey asal

hood kâput

hornet zanbur-e sorkh

horse asb; **horse and cart** asb ve gâri; **horse racing** mosâbeghe-ye asb; asb davâni; **horseback riding** asb savâri

hose shilang

hospital bimârestân

hostage gerôgân

hostel hostel

hot garm; dâgh; **hot water** âb-e garm

hotel hotel; **hotel industry** sanâ'ye-ye hoteldâri

hour sâ'at

house khâne

housing estate/project shahrak

how? chetur?; che juri?; **how are you?** cheturi?; **how near?** cheghadr nazdik?; **how far?** cheghadr dur?; **how many?** chand (tâ)?; **how much/ many?** cheghadr?; **how much?** *price* chand?

human rights hoghugh-e bashar

humanitarian aid komak-e ensâni

hundred sad

hungry gorosne; **I'm hungry.** Man gorosname.; Man gorosne hastam.

hurry: **I am in a hurry.** Ajale dâram.
husband shôhar
hygiene hefz-o-seha

I

I man
ice yakh; **ice ax/ice pick** yakhshekan; **ice-box** yakh-châl; **ice-cream** bastani
illiterate bisavâd
imam emâm
in dar; **in front of** jelô; **in the morning** sobh; **in the afternoon** ba'd az zohr; **in the evening** asr; **in front of** pish-e ruye
included shâmel; shâmel shode
independence esteghlâl
independent mostaghel; **independent state** keshvar-e mostaghel
index finger angosht-e neshân
India Hendustân
Indian Hendi
indicator light râhnamâ
indigestion rudel
industrial estate mantegheye san'ati
industry san'at; sanâye
infant kudak; bache
infected: It is infected. Ofuniyat karde.
infection ofuniyat
influenza ânfluenzâ
information etelâ'ât; **information office** daftar-e etelâ'ât
ink jôhar
inner tube lule-ye dâkheli
inquiries morâje'ât
insect hashare; jânevar;

insects hasharât; **insect repellant** hashare-kosh
insecticide hashare-kosh
inside tu
insurance bime; **insurance policy** gharârdâd-e bime
internal dâkheli; **internal flight** parvâz-e dâkheli
international baynolmelali; **international flight** parvâz-e baynolmelali; **international operator** operâtor-e baynolmelali
internet internet; **internet café** kafe internet
intestine(s) rude(-hâ)
invade tâkhtotâz kardan
Iran Irân
Iranian *person* Irâni
Iranian Red Crescent Sazemân-e Anjoman-e Helâl-e Ahmar-e Irân
Iraq Arâgh
Iraqi Arâghi
Ireland Irland
Irish Irlandi
iron *metal* âhan *for clothes* utu
irrigation âbyâri
Islam Eslâm
Islamic Eslâmi
Israeli Esrâ'ili
it ô; u
I.T. kâmpyuter
Italian Italiyâ'i
itch: It itches here. Injâ mikhârad.

J

jack jâk
jackal shaghal
jacket kôt
jam morabâ
January Zhânviye

Japan Zhâpân
Japanese Zhâpâni
jaw fak
jazz jâz
jeans jinz
jelly *jam* morabâ
jewelry javâher
Jewish Yahudi
jihad jehâd
joiner najâr
joint mafsal
journalist khabar-negâr
judge ghâzi
jug pârch
July Zhu'iye
jumper boluz
June Zhu'an
just now hamin al'ân

K

kebab kabâb
ketchup sôs
kettle ketri
key kelid
kidney koliye; **kidneys** koliye-hâ
kilim gelim
kill koshtan
killer âdamkosh; ghâtel
kilogram kilogrâm
kilometer kilometr
king malek
kiosk kyosk
Kirgiz Kirghiz
Kirgizstan Kirghizestân
knee zânu
knife kârd/châghu
know dânestan
Kurd Kord

L

ladder nardebân
lady's fingers *okra* bâmiye
lake daryâche
lamb bare; *meat* gusht-e bare
lamp cherâgh
landslide âbroft
language zabân
laptop computer kâmpyuter
last âkhari; **last night** dishab; **last week** hafte-ye gozashte; **last year** pârsâl
laundry khoshk-shu'i
law ghânun; **law court** dâdgâh
lawyer vakil
laziness tambali
leader rahbar
leaf barg
learn yâd gereftan; **to learn by heart** az bar yâd gereftan
learn yâdgereftan
leather charm
left chap; **left-hand** dast-e chap; **left-wing** chapi
leg pâ
leisure industry senf-e tafri-hâti
lemon limu; **lemon squash** sharbat-e limu
lens lenz
lentils adas
Leo Asad
leopard palang
less kamtar
lesson dars
letter yek nâme
lettuce kâhu
liberate âzâd kardan; rahâ kardan
liberation âzâdi
liberty âzâdi
Libra Mizân

library ketâbkhâne
lice shepesh(-hâ)
lie dorugh
lieutenant sotvân; **lieutenant-colonel** sarhang dovum; **lieutenant-general** sartip
life zendegi
lift âsânsur
light *noun* nur; *electric* cherâgh; *adjective: not heavy* sabok
lightbulb lâmp
lightning bargh; **lightning bolt** mile-ye barghgir
limbs andâm-hâ
lime limu sabz
line khat
lion shir
lip lab
lipstick matik
liter litr
literature adabiyât
little kuchek; **a little bit** yek (meghdâr-e) kam
live *verb* zendegi kardan
liver jigar
livestock chahâr pâyân-e asli
lizard susmâr
loaf nân-e sândvich
local mahali; **a local shop for local people** dôkân-e mahali barâye mardom-e mahali
loose change pul-e khord
loot ghârat kardan
lorry kâmyon; terayli
lose gom kardan
louse shepesh
love *verb* dust dâshtan
low pâ'in; kutâh; **low blood pressure** feshâr-e pâ'in
lower house majles-e bâlâ

luggage bâr
lunch nâhâr
lung shosh

M

machine mâshin; **machine gun** mosalsal
madrasa madrase
magazine majale
mailbox sandugh posti
main asli; **main square** maydân-e asli
maize zorat
major-general sarlashkar
majority aksariyat
man; male mard
mango mângô
manure kud
many ziyâd
map naghshe; **map of Tehran** naghshe-ye Tehrân
March Mârs
mare mâdiyân
margarine mârjârin
marital status vaz'iyat-e ezdevâji
market bâzâr
marketing bâzâr yâbi
married *female* shôhardâr; *male* mota'ahel
marsh mordâb
martyr shahid
mascara rimmel
match mosâbeghe
material pârche
maternity hospital bimârestân-e hâmele
maths riyâzi
mattress toshak
May Mey
me man
meadow marghzâr
meal ghazâ; **meals** ghazâ-hâ

meat gusht
mechanic mekânik
media resâne-hâ
meet molâghat kardan
meeting molâghât
melon kharboze
memory hefz
menu menyu
mercenary sarbâz-e mozdur
metal felez
meter metr
metro (tunel-e) zir zamin; metro
microscope mikroskop
midnight nim-e shab
midwife ghâbela
mile mâyl
military *adjective* nezâmi
milk *noun* shir; *cow's* shir-e gâv; *goat's* shir-e boz; *powdered* shir-e pudr; *mother's* shir-e mâdar; *verb: an animal* dushidan
mill âsyâb
millet arzan
million milyôn
mine *explosive* min; **mines** min-hâ; **anti-personnel mine** zed-e personel; **mine: anti-tank mine** zed-e tânk; **mine detector** min yâb; **mine disposal** minbardâri
minefield mantaghe-ye min
mineral water âb-e ma'dani
minister vazir
ministry vezârat; **Ministry of Agriculture** Vezârat-e Keshâvarzi; **Ministry of Commerce** Vezârat-e Tejârat; **Ministry of Culture** Vezârat-e Farhang; **Ministry of**

Defense Vezârat-e Defâ'; **Ministry of Education** Vezârat-e Âmuzesh va Parvaresh; **Ministry of Finance** Vezârat-e Eghtesâd; **Ministry of Foreign Affairs** Vezârat-e Omur-e Khâreji; **Ministry of Health** Vezârat-e Behdâsht; **Ministry of Home Affairs** Vezârat-e Keshvar; **Ministry of Information** Vezârat-e Etelâ'ât; **Ministry of Justice** Vezârat-e Dâdgostari; **Ministry of Tourism** Vezârat-e Turizm
minority aghaliyat; **minority vote** ra'y-e aghaliyat
mint na'nâ
minute daghighe
mirror âyene
Miss Khânom
missile mushak
mist meh
misty meh
modem môdem
modern modern
mole *animal* kurmush
Monday Dôshambe
money pul
mongoose peshak-e vahshi
monkey maymun
month mâh
monument âsâr
moon mâh
more bishtar
morning sobh; **good morning!** sobh be khayr!; **in the morning** sobh; **this morning** emruz sobh
mortar khompâre
mosque masjed; **Friday mosque** masjed-e Jom'e

mosquito

mosquito(es) pashe(-hâ); **mosquito net** pashakhâne

mother mâdar

motorbike motor

mountain kuh; **mountain pass** gozargâh-e kuhi; **mountain range** selsele-ye kuhi

mouse mush

mouth dehan; **mouthwash** mâye'-ye shostoshu-ye dehan

move harekat kardan; **Do not move!** Harekat nakonid!

Mr. Âghâ

Mrs. Khânom

mulberry tut

mule ghâter

multiplication zarb

multiply zarb kardan

munitions mohemât

murder ghatl

muscle azule

museum muze

mushroom qârch

music musigh(i)

Muslim Mosalmân

mustache sebil

mustard khardal

mutton gusht-e gusfand

N

nail of finger/toe nâkhon; metal mikh; **nail polish** lâk; **nail-clippers** nâkhon-gir

name esm; nâm

napkin dastmâl

narrow bârik

nation melat

nationalism vatanparasti

nationalist vatanparast

nationality meliyat; tâbe'iy-at

natural disaster mosibat-e tabi'i

navel nâf

navy artesh-e daryâ'i

near nazdik

neck gardan

necklace gardanband

necktie kerâvât

nectarine shalil

need ehtiyâj

needle suzan

negotiator miyânjigar-e mozâkerât

nerve asab

neutral drive dande-ye khalâs

new nô; **new moon** helâl-e mâh; **New Year** Nô Ruz

New Zealand Zeland-e Naw

newborn child bache nô-zâd

newspaper ruznâme; **newspaper in English** ruznâme be zabân-e Ingilisi

newsstand kyosk-e ruznâme

next ba'di; **next week** hafte-ye ba'd; hafte-ye dige; **next year** sâl-e âyande

night shab; **good night!** shab be khayr!; **last night** dishab

nightclub disko

nightingale bolbol

nine noh

nineteen nuzdah

ninety navad

ninth nôhom

no nah; nakhyr; **no ice, please** bedun-e yakh, lotfan; **no sugar, please** bidun-e shekar, lotfan;

paint

no entry vorud mamnu' (ast); no problem! moshkeli nist?; no smoking sigâr keshidan mamnu' ast

noise sedâ
noisy por-e sarsedâ
noon zohr
north shomâl
Northern Ireland Irland-e Shomâli
nose bini; damâgh
not na-/ne-; not enough kam
notebook daftarche
novel român; a novel in English român be zabân-e Ingilisi
November Novambr
now al'ân; hâlâ; just now hamin al'ân
nuclear atomi; nuclear energy niru-ye âtomi; nuclear power station nirugâh-e âtomi
nurse parastâr
nut almond bâdâm

O

objective maghsud
observer moshâhede konande
October Oktôbr
of -e; -ye
office edâre; daftar
office worker kârmand
officer afsar
oil rôghan; oilcan ghuti-ye rôghan
ointment cream rôghan; krem
okay! khob!
okra bâmiye

old people pir; things kohne; old man âghâ-ye mosen; old woman khânom-e mosen old city shahr-e ghadimi
olive(s) zaytun
on bâlâ-ye; ru
once yekbâr
one yek; one-quarter rob'; one-third yek sevom; one-half nesf; one-way street khiyâbân-e yek tarafe
onion(s) piyâz
open bâz
opera operâ; opera house tâlâr-e operâ
operating theatre/room otâgh-e amaliyât
operator operâtor
opponent mokhâlef
opposite ru-be-ru
opposition mokhâlefin
or yâ
orange portoghâl
orchard bâgh-e mive
organ of body ozv
orphan yatim
Orthodox Ortodoks
ounce âns
outlet commercial forushgâh
outside birun
overcoat pâlto
owl buf
ox gâv-e nar
oxygen âksizhen

P

padlock ghofl
page safhe
pain dard; painkiller mosaken
paint rang

Pakistan

Pakistan Pâkestân
Pakistani Pâkestâni
palm *of hand* kaf-e dast
pancreas lôz-ul-me'de
pantyhose jurâb shalvâri
paper kâghaz; *article* maghâle; **a piece of paper** yek tike kâghaz
parachute parashut
parcel yek baste
park pârk
parliament majles; **parliament building** sâkhtemân-e majles
parrot tuti
partridge kabk
party *celebration* mehmâni; *political* hezb
pass *an exam* ghabul shodan
passenger savâri
passport pâsport; **passport number** shomâre-ye pâsport
past gozashte
pasta mâkâroni
path râh
patrol gasht
peace solh; **to make peace** solh kardan; **peace-keeping troops** lashkar-e hâfez solh
peach holu
peacock tâvus
peak nôk
peanuts bâdâm-e zamini
pear golâbi
peas nokhod sabz
pediatrician doktur-e atfâl
pen ghalam; khodkâr
pencil madâd
penknife châghu-ye kucheke jibi
people mardom

pepper felfel
perfume atr
Persian Fârsi
person âdam; mard
personal shakhsi
personnel *military* setâd
petrol benzin
pharmacy dârukhâne
pheasant gharghâvol
phone telefôn; **cell phone** telefôn-e dasti
photocopier dastgâh-e fotokopi
photocopy fotokopi
photograph aks
photography aks var dâri
physiotherapy fiziyoterâpi
pick up bardâshtan
pickaxe kolang
pickles torshi
piece tike
pig khuk
pigeon kabutar
pillow bâlesht
pilot khalebân
pin sanjâgh; **pins and needles: I have pins and needles in my ...** ...-am khâb rafte.
pink surati
Pisces Hut
pistachio peste
pistol tapânche
pitch zamin-e futbol
pizza pitsa
place mahal; **place of birth** mahal-e tavalod
placenta joft
plain(s) dasht
plane havâpaymâ
planet sayâre
plank takhte
plant *noun* giyâh; *verb* kâshtan

plaster *cast* palâster; *Band-aid* chasp
plastic pelâstik
plate boshghâb
platform saku; **platform number** shomâre-ye saku
please! befarmâ'id!
plow gâv-e âhan
plow shokhm zadan
plug *bath* plâg; *electric two-pin* dô-shâkhe; *three-pin* seh-shâkhe
plum âlu
pocket jib
podium sakn
police polis; **police station** kalântari
polite mo'adab
political siyâsi; **political analyst** rizhehgar-e olum-e siyâsi
politician siyâsatmadâr
politics siyâsat
pomegranate anâr
pond hôz
pony kore-ye asb
pop music musighi-ye pâp
portable T.V. televizyon-e dasti
Portuguese Portagâli
post post
post office postkhâne
postcard kârt postâl
pot kuza
potato(oes) sib zamini; **sweet potato** kachâlu
pottery kuzehgari
poultry morghân-e khânegi
pound *weight* pond; **pound sterling** pond-e esterling
powder pudr
pregnant hâmele; **I'm pregnant.** Man hâmele hastam.

present *gift* kâdô; *time* hâl-e hâzer; zamân-e hâzer
president ra'is jomhur
pressure cooker zud paz
prime minister nâkhost vazir
printer printer
prison zendân
prisoner asir; **to take prisoner** asir kardan; **prisoner-of-war** asir-e jangi; **prisoner-of-war camp** ordu-ye asirân-e jangi
problem moshkel; **no problem!** moshkeli nist?
profession shoghl
program *computer* barnâme (-ye kâmpyuter)
progress pishraft
projector prozhektar
protest *noun* mokhâlefat; e'terâz
provisions ghazâ
pump pâmp
pumpkin kadu tanbel
punish tanbih kardan
pupil *school* shâgerd; *of eye* mardomak-e chesm
purple benafsh
pursue ta'ghib kardan

Q

quail baldarchin
question so'âl
quick sari'; tond
quiet sâket; **keep quiet!** sâket!

R

rabbit khargush
rabies hâri
radiator râdyâtor

radio

radio radyô; **radio taxi** tâksi telefôni

radish torobche

raid tâkht o tâz

railway râh âhan; **railway station** istgâh-e ghatâr

rain bârân; **It is raining.** Bârân miyâd.

rainbow rangin kamân

raincoat bârâni

raisins keshmesh

ram ghuch

Ramadan Ramazân

rash jush

rat mush-e sahrâ'i

ravine dare-tand; darband

raw khâm

razor blade tigh

read khândan

ready hâzer; **I am ready.** Hâzer am.

reap darô kardan

reason dalil; **reason for travel** dalil-e safar

receipt resid

record safe

red ghermez; **Red Crescent** Helâl-e Ahmar; **Red Cross** Salib-e Sorkh

referee dâvar

refugee panâhande; **refugees** panâhandegân; **refugee camp** kâmp-e panâhandegân

regiment hang

registered mail post-e sefâreshi

reinforcements niru-ye komaki

relative fâmil

relief emdâdi; **relief aid** komak-e emdâdi; **relief worker** kârmand-e emdâdi

religion din

repeat tekrâr kardan

report gozâresh

reserved rezerv shode

resist esteghâmat kardan

restaurant rasturân

retail industry senf-e khorda forushi

retreat aghab neshini kardan

reverse dande aghab

revolution enghelâb

rib dande

ribcage ghafase-ye sine

rice: *uncooked* berenj; *cooked* polav

rifle tofang

right râst; **right hand** dast-e râst; **right-wing** jenâh râst; **You are right.** Râst migid.

ring halghe

ripe reside

river rudkhâne; **river bank** lab-e rudkhâne

road râh; jâde; khiyâbân; **road map** naghshe-ye râh; **roadblock** râh-bandân

robbery dozdi

rock sang

rocket mushak; râket; **rocket-launcher** saku-ye partâb-e mushak

roof bâm

room otâgh; **room number** shomâre-ye otâgh

rooster khorus

root rishe

rope tanâb

rosary tasbih

rose gol

roundabout maydân

rubber lâstik; *eraser* pâk-

kon; **rubber boots** putinhâ
ruble rubel
rude bitarbiyat
rug ghâli; ghâliche
rugby râgbi
ruins âsâr
ruler *instrument* khatkesh
run davidan
Russia Rus
Russian Rusi
rust zang
rye gandom-e siyâh

S

sack guni
safety amniyat; **safety pin**
sanjogh ghofli
Sagittarius Ghôs
saint's tomb gur-e moghadas
salad sâlâd
sales forushendagi
saliva âb-e dehan
salt namak
salty shur
sand mâse
sand shen
sandal(s) sandal(-hâ)
sandwich sândvich
sanitary towels jan pâk
satchel kif(-e madrase)
satellite phone telefôn-e
mâhvâre
Saturday Shambe
sauce sôs
saucer na'lbaki
sausage sôsis
saw are
scanner eskaner
scarf shâlgardan
school madrase
scientist dâneshmand

scissors ghaychi
Scorpio Aghrab
scorpion aghrab
Scotland Eskâtland
Scottish Eskâtlandi
screw pich
screwdriver pichkoshti
season fasl
seat sandali; *in assembly*
korsi
second dôvom; *of time*
sâniye
secret police polis-e seri
secretary monshi
security amniyat
see didan; **see you tomorrow!** tâ fardâ!
seeds tokhm
September Septambr
session jalase
seven haft
seventeen hivdah
seventh haftom
seventy haftâd
sewing machine mâshin
khayâti
shampoo shâmpu
shaving cream krem-e
rish
shawl shâl
she u; ô
sheep gusfand
sheepdog sag-e gale
sheet malâfe; *of paper*
varaghe
shelf tâghche
shelter panâhgâh
Shi'ism Shi'a
Shi'ite Shi'i; Ahl-e Shi'a
shirt pirâhan
shoe kafsh; **shoes** kafsh-hâ;
shoeshop kafsh forushi;
to shoe *a horse* na'l kardan

shoot

shoot shelik kardan; **Don't shoot!** Shelik nakonid!; **to shoot down** hadaf gharâr dâdan
shop maghâze; dôkân
shopping kharid
short *things* kutâh; *people* ghad kutâh
shoulder shâne
shoulder-blade ostokhun-e shâne
shower dush; *of rain* ragbâr
shrapnel shrapnel; tarkesh
shrine ziyâratgâh
shut baste
sick mariz
side *of body* taraf
sidestreet kuche
siege mohâsere
sieve âbkesh
sign neshâni
signature emzâ
silence sokut
silk abrisham
silken abrishami
silkworm(s) kerm-e abrisham
silver noghre
single mojarad
sister khâhar
sit neshastan
six shesh
sixteen shânzdah
sixth sheshom
sixty shast
size andâze
skiing eski
skin pust
skull jomjome; kâse-ye sar
sky âsemân
slate lôh
sleep *noun* khâb; *verb* khâbidan
sleeping bag kise khâb
sleeping car *of train* vâgon-e takhtkhâbdâr
sleeping pill ghors-e khâb
slope dâmane
slow yavâsh
small kuchek
smell bu; *verb* bu dâdan; **to smell** *something* bu kardan
smoking: no smoking sigâr keshidan mamnu' ast
snail halazun
snake mâr; **snakebite** nish-e mâr
snow barf; **It is snowing.** Barf miyâd
snowblindness barf kuri
snowdrift barf-e anbâshta
snowflakes dane-ye barf
soap sâbun
soccer futbol; **soccer match** mosâbeghe-ye futbol
socialism sosyâlizm
socialist sosyâlist
socks jurâb
soft narm
soil khâk
soldier sarbâz
sole *of foot* kaf-e pâ; *of shoe* zir(-e kafsh)
son pesar
sore throat/tonsils gelu dard/tânsal
soup sup
sour torsh
south jonub
souvenir shop soghât forushi
sow afshândan
spade bil
Spain Espâniyâ
Spanish Espâniyâ'i
spanner âchâr
spare tyre/tire lâstik-e ezâfe
sparrow gonjeshk
speak harf zadan

speak: **Do you speak Farsi?**
(Âyâ) shomâ Fârsi bala-
did?; **I speak Farsi.** Man
Fârsi baladam.
speaker sokhanrân
specialist motakhases
speed harârat
spice adviye
spicy *hot* tond
spider ankabut
spinach esfenâj
spinal column; spine naxâ'
sponge esfânj
spoon ghâshogh
spring *of water* sarchesme;
season bahâr
spy jâsus
squirrel sanjâb
stadium estadyum
staff *military* setâd-e artesh
stag gavazn-e nar
stairs pele
stale mânde
stallion asb-e nar
stamp tambr
stand istâdan
star setâre; **stars** setâre-
gân
start shuru' kardan
state *nation* dôlat
station istgâh
stationer's store forushgâh-
e lavâzem-e tahrir
stationery lavâzem-e tahrir
statue mojasame
steel fulâd
steering wheel farmân
stethoscope gushi-ye tebi
stick asâ
stomach shekam
stomachache deldard
stone sang
stool chârpâye
stop motavaghef kardan;
stop! vâ'isin!

store maghâze
storm tufân
stove gâz; *(hob)* cherâgh;
cooking fer-e khorâk
pazi; *heating* bukhâri
straight on mostaghim
straw kâh
strawberries tut farangi
stream rud; juy-e âb
street khiyâbân
string nakh
strong ghavi
struggle *noun* kushesh; ejtehâd
student *university* dâneshju
sturgeon sag-e mâhi; mâhi-
ye khâvyâr
subject mavzu'
submachine gun mosalsal-e
khodkâr
subtract menhâ kardan
subtraction menhâ
suburb home
subway *metro* (tunel-e) zir
zamin; metro
success movafaghiyat
sugar shekar; **sugarlump**
ghand; **no sugar, please**
bidun-e shekar, lotfan
suit kot-o-shalvâr
suitcase chamedân
sum hesâb
summer tâbestân
summit nôk; ghale
sun âftâb
sunblock cream krem-e
âftâb gereftan
Sunday Yekshambe
sunglasses aynak âftâbi
Sunni Soni; Ahl-e Sonat
Sunnism Sonat
sunny: It is sunny. Âftâb
miyâd.
sunrise tolu'

sunset ghorub-e âftâb
sunstroke âftâb zadegi
supermarket super
supper shâm
surgeon jarâh
surgery *operation* amaliyât; amal
surname esm-e fâmil; nâm-e khândevâdegi
surrender taslim kardan
surround ahâte kardan
swamp mordâb
sweater boluz
sweet shirin
swimming shenâ
switchboard operator telefônchi
syringe sôranj
syrup sharbat

T

table miz; **tablecloth** *table* rumizi; *floor* sofre
tailor khayât
Tajik Tâjik
Tajikistan Tâjikistân
take gereftan; **to take shelter** panâh bordan; **take-away food/take-out food** ghazâ-ye ke bâ khod mibarand
talk *noun* sohbat; *verb* sohbat kardan
tall boland
tank tânk
tape *cassette* navâr; **tape recorder** zabt
tarmac road jâde-ye âsfâlt
taste *noun* cheshâyi
tasteless bi maze
tasty khosh maze
Taurus Sôr
tea chây; **tea with lemon** chây bâ limu; **tea with milk** chây bâ shir; **tea without milk** chây bidun-e shir
teach yâd dâdan
teacher mo'alem
tea-glass estekân
teahouse châykhâne
team tim
teapot ghuri
teaspoon ghâshogh chây khuri
teenager nôjavân
teeth dandân-hâ
telecommunications mokhâberât
telephone telefôn; **mobile phone/cell phone** telefôn-e dasti; **telephone center** markaz-e telefôn/mokhâberât
telescope teleskop
television televizyon
temperature tab
temple ma'bad
ten dah
tender narm
tent châdor; **tent pegs** gire-ye châdor
tenth dahom
termite muryâne
test *academic: noun* emtehân; âzemun; *verb* emtehân/âzemun kardan
testify govâhi dâdan; shehâdat dâdan
thank you! mersi!; motashakeram!; tashakor!; khayli mamnun!
that ân
thaw âb shodan
theatre te'âtr
theft dozdi
therapist terâpist

there ânjâ; **is there?** hast?; **are there?** hastand?
thermometer damâsanj
these inhâ
they ânhâ; ishân
thief dozd
thigh rân
thimble angoshtâne
third sevom
thirsty teshne; **I'm thirsty.** Man teshname. *or* Man teshne hastam.
thirteen sizdah
thirty si
this in
thorax (ghafase-ye) sine
those ânhâ
thousand hezâr
thread nakh
three seh; **three times** sehbâr; **three-quarters** seh rob'; **three days before** seh ruz pish; **three days from now** seh ruz dige
throat gelu
throw andâkhtan
thumb shast
thunder ra'd
thunderstorm ra'd o bargh
Thursday Panjshambe
tibia ghasaba'i kubrâ
tick *insect* kane
ticket bilit; **ticket office** edâre-ye forush-e bilit
tie kerâvât
tights jurâb shalvâri
time vaght
timetable jadval-e safar
tire *of car* lâstik
tissues dastmâl kâghazi
to be; tâ
today emruz
toe angosht-e pâ

toilet(s) tuvâlet(-hâ); **toilet paper** dastmâl kâghazi; dastmâl tuvâlet; **ladies/gents toilets** tuvâlet-e zanâne/tuvâlet-e mardâne
toiletries lavâzem-e ârâyesh
tomato gôje farangi
tomb gur
tomorrow fardâ; **tomorrow morning** fardâ sobh; **tomorrow afternoon** fardâ ba'd az zohr; **tomorrow night** fardâ shab
ton; tonne ton
tongue zabân
tonight emshab
too *very much* khayli; **too little** kam; **too much/too many** ziyâd
tools afzâr
tooth dandân; **teeth** dandân-hâ; **toothache** dandân dard; **toothbrush** mesvâk; **toothpaste** khamir dandân; **toothpick** khalâl dandân
top bâlâ
torrent saylâb
torture shekanje
tough *meat* seft
tourism *activity* sayâhat; turizm; *industry* sanâ'ye-ye jehângardi
tourist turist
tow rope sim-e boksol
towel hôle
tower borj
town shahr; **town center** markaz-e shahr; **town map** naghshe-ye shahr
trachea ghasaba ar-ri'a
tractor terâktôr

trade union etehâdiye-ye asnâf
trader tâjer
traditional sonati
traffic lights cheragh ghermez
trailer terayli
train station estishan; istgâh-e ghatâr
tranquilizer mosâken
transfer *to put through on the phone* vasl kardan
transformer trânsformer
translation tarjome
translator motarjem
travel safar; jehângardi; **travel agency** âzhâns-e mosâferat
traveler's checks terâvel-chek-hâ
tray sini
treacle shire
treasury khazâne
tree derakht
troops sarbâzân
trousers shalvâr
truce solh
truck kâmyon; terayli
true dorost
trunk *of tree* tane; *of car* sandogh-e aghab
truth haghighat
tuberculosis sel
Tuesday Sehshambe
turkey morgh-e hendi
Turkey Torkiye
Turkish Tork
Turkmen Torkaman
Turkmenistan Torkaman-estân
turn: **turn left** dast-e chap bepich; **turn right** dast-e râst bepich
turnip shalgham

twelve davâzdah
twentieth bistom
twenty bist
twice dôbâr
twins dô-ghulu
two dô
two-thirds dô sevom
typewriter mâshin-tahrir
tyre lâstik

U

umbilical cord band-e nâf
umbilicus nâf
umbrella chatr
uncomfortable nârâhat
uncooked nâpokhte
under zir
underground *metro* (tunel-e) zir zamin; metro
understand fahmidan
underwear zirpush
unexploded: **unexploded bomb** bomb-e monfajer nashode; **unexploded ammunition/ordnance** mohemât-e monfajer nashode
unhappy nârâhat
uniform uniform
United Nations Sâzemân-e Melal-e Motahed
university dâneshgâh
until tâ
up bâlâ; **up to** tâ
upper house majles-e pâ'in
urine miz
us mâ
USA Âmrikâ
Uzbek Ozbek
Uzbekistan Ozbekistân

V

valley dare
van vânet

varnish vârni; vârnish
vase goldân
vegetable(s) sabzi; sabzijât;
 vegetable shop sabzi
 forushi
vegetarian: I am a vegetarian. Man giyah-khuram.
vein rag
veranda terâs
vertebra fighra
very khayli; **very cold** khayli
 sard; **very hot** khayli
 garm
vest *undershirt* zirpush
veto *noun* rad; *verb* rad kardan
victory piruzi
videotape kaset vidyô; **videotape player** navâr vidyô
view manzare
village deh
vinegar serke
violence khoshunat
viper tirmâr
Virgo Sunbule
visa viza
vitamins vitâmin-hâ
voltage regulator adâptar
volunteer dâvatalab
vomit estefrâgh kardan
vote *noun* ra'y; **vote-rigging**
 takhalof-e ra'y
voting ra'y dâdan
vulture lâshkhur

W

waist kamar
waistcoat *jacket with
 sleeves* zhâkat; *jacket
 without sleeves* jelighe
wake up bidâr shodan
Wales Vaylz
walk ghadam zadan
walking stick asâ

wall divâr
wallet kif-e pul
walnut gerdu
want khâstan
war jang
warm garm
washing powder pudr-e
 lebâs shu'i
wasp zanbur
watch sâ'at
watchmaker's sâ'at sâz
water âb; **water bottle** botri-
 ye âb
waterfall âb shâr
watermelon hendevâne
way râh; **this way** in var;
 that way ân var
we mâ
weak za'if
weapon aslahe
weather havâ
wedding arusi
Wednesday Chahârshambe
week hafte; **last week** hafte-
 ye gozashte; **this week** in
 hafte; **next week** hafte-ye
 ba'd; hafte-ye dige
welcome! khôsh âmadid!;
 you're welcome! befarmâ'id!
well khob; *healthy* sâlem; *of
 water* chesm; **well!**
 khob!
Welsh Ahl-e Vaylz
west gharb
what? che?; chi?; **what's
 that?** ân chi-ye?
wheat gandom
wheelchair sandali-ye charkhdâr
when? kay?
where? kojâ?; **where is?**
 kojâ-st?; **where are?**
 kojâ-nd?

which? kodâm?
white sefid
who? ki?; **who are you?** shomâ ki hastid?
why? cherâ?
wide pahn
wife zan; khânom
win bordan
wind bâd
window panjere
windpipe ghasaba ar-ri'a
windscreen/windshield shishe; **windscreen wipers** barf pâk-kon
windy: It is windy. Bâd miyâd.
wine sharâb
winter zemestân
wire sim
with bâ; **with ice** bâ yakh
without bedun-e
wolf gorg
woman zan; **women** zanân
womb rahem
wood *substance* chub; *of trees* jangal
wool pashm
work kâr
work kâr kardan
worm(s) kerm(-hâ)
wound majruh kardan
wrench âchâr

wrestling koshti
wrist moch-e dast
write neveshtan
writer nevisande
writing paper kâghaz barâye neveshtan
wrong: You are wrong. Eshtebâh mikonid.

Y

yard *measurement* yârd
year sâl; **the year before last** piyârsâl; **last year** pârsâl; **this year** emsâl; **next year** sâl-e âyande; **the year after next** dô sâl dige
yellow zard
yes bale
yesterday diruz; **yesterday morning** diruz sobh; **yesterday afternoon** diruz ba'd az zohr; **yesterday night** dishab
yogurt mâst
you *singular* tô; *plural/ formal* shomâ
young javân

Z

zero sefr
zipper zip
zoo bâgh-e vahsh

FARSI
Phrasebook

1. ETIQUETTE

ADAB

Hello!	**Salâm!**
—the response is:	**Salâm!**
How are you?	**Cheturi?**
Fine, thank you!	**Khob!**
Good morning!	**Sobh be khayr!***
Good afternoon!	**Roz be khayr!***
Good evening!	**Shab tân khosh!***
Good night!	**Shab be khayr!***
See you later!	**Tâ fardâ!**
—the response is:	**Khodâ hâfez!**
See you tomorrow!	**Tâ fardâ!**
—the response is:	**Tâ fardâ, inshallâh!**
Goodbye!	**Khodâ hâfez!**
—the response is:	**Khodâ hâfez!**
Bon voyage!	**Safar be khayr!**
Welcome!	**Khosh âmadid!**
Please!	**Khâhesh mikonam!**
Please sit down!	**Befarmâ'id, beshinid!**
Please eat!	**Befarmâ'id!**
Thank you!	**Mersi!**

* You reply with the same greeting.

2. QUICK REFERENCE
MARJA'-YE TOND

I	**man**
you *singular*	**tô**
he/she/it	**u; ô**
we	**mâ**
you *plural*	**shomâ**
they	**ânhâ; ishân**
yes	**bale**
no	**na**
this	**in**
that	**ân**
these	**inhâ**
those	**ânhâ**
here	**injâ**
there	**ânjâ**
where?	**kojâ?**
who?	**ki?**
what?	**chi?; che?**
when?	**kay?**
which?	**kodâm?**
how?	**chetur?; che juri?**
why?	**cherâ?**
how far?	**cheghadar dur?**
how near?	**cheghadar nazdik?**
how much?	**cheghadar?**
how much *(price)*?	**chand?**
how many?	**chand (tâ)?**
what's that?	**ân chi-ye?**

is there?	**hast?**
are there?	**hastand?**
where is?	**kojâ-st?**
where are?	**kojâ-nd?**
here is ...	**... injâ-st.**
here are ...	**... injâ-nd.**
What must I do?	**Che kâr bâyad bokonam?**
What do you want?	**Chi mikhâ'id?**
very	**khayli**
and	**va; o**
or	**yâ**
but	**amâ; vali**
I like ...	**Man ... dust dâram**
I don't like ...	**Man ... dust nadâram**
I want ...	**... mikhâham**
I want to ...	**Mikhâham ...**
I don't want ...	**... nemikhâham**
I don't want to ...	**Nemikhâham ...**
I know.	**Midânam.**
I don't know.	**Nemidânam.**
Do you understand?	**Mifahmid?**
I understand.	**Mifahmam.**
I don't understand.	**Nemifahmam.**
Excuse me!	**Bebakhshid!**
Sorry!	**Bebakhshid, ma'zerat mikhâm!**
My condolences! *(if someone has died)*	**Tasliyat migam!**
I am grateful.	**Az zahmatetun khayli motashakeram.**
It's important.	**Mohem ast.**
It doesn't matter.	**Ayb nadâre.**
No problem!	**Moshkeli nist!**

more or less	**kam o bish**
Is everything okay?	**Hame chi dorost-e?**
Danger!	**Khatar!**
Could you repeat that?	**Mishe ânra tekrâr konid?**
How do you spell that?	**Chejuri heji-sh mikonid?**

I am cold.	**Man sard-am-e.**
I am hot.	**Man garm-am-e.**
I am right.	**Man râst miguyam.**
I am sleepy.	**Man khâb-am miyâd.**
I am hungry.	**Man gorosnam-e.**
I am thirsty.	**Man teshnam-e.**
I am angry.	**Man asabâni-yam.**
I am happy.	**Man khoshhâl-am.**
I am sad.	**Man nârâht-am.**
I am tired.	**Man khaste-yam.**
I am well.	**Man khob-am.**

—Colors   Rang-ha

black	**siyâh; meshki**
blue	**âbi**
navy blue	**sorme'i**
turquoise blue	**firuze'i**
brown	**ghahve'i**
color	**rang**
green	**sabz**
grey	**khâkastari**
orange	**nârenji**
pink	**surati**
purple	**banafsh**
red	**qermez**
white	**sefid**
yellow	**zard**

3. INTRODUCTIONS
MOGHABELAT

What is your name?	**Esm-e shomâ chi-ye?**
My name is ...	**Esm-e man ... ast.**
May I introduce you to ...	**Shomâ râ bâ ... mo'arefi konam.**
This is my ...	**In ...-e man ast.**
friend	**dust**
traveling companion	**hamsafar**
colleague	**hamkâr**
relative	**fâmil**

TITLES — "Mr." is **Âghâ** and "Mrs." or "Miss" is **Khânom**, and can be used with people's first names, e.g. **Âghâ-ye Fred** and **Khânom-e Emma**. When you don't know a person's name, you can also use these for the English forms of address "Sir" and "Madam".

—Nationality
Meliyat

Iran	**Irân**
—Iranian *person*	**—Irâni**
Where are you from?	**Shomâ ahl-e kojâ hastid?**
I am from ...	**Man az ... hastam.**
America	**Âmrikâ**
Australia	**Ostrâlyâ**
Britain	**Baritânyâ; Ingilis**
Canada	**Kânâdâ**
China	**Chin**
England	**Ingilis**
Europe	**Urupâ**
Germany	**Âlmân**

India	**Hendustân**
Ireland	**Irland**
Japan	**Zhâpân**
New Zealand	**Zeland-e Nô**
Northern Ireland	**Irland-e Shomâli**
Pakistan	**Pâkestân**
Russia	**Rus**
Wales	**Vaylz**
Scotland	**Eskâtland**
the USA	**Âmrikâ**
I am ...	**Man ... -am/-yam.**
American	**Âmrikâ'i**
Australian	**Ostrâlyâ'i**
British	**Ingilisi**
Canadian	**Kânâdâ'i**
Chinese	**Chini**
Dutch	**Holândi**
English	**Inglisi**
French	**Farânsavi**
German	**Âlemâni**
Indian	**Hendi**
Irish	**Irlandi**
Israeli	**Esrâ'ili**
Japanese	**Zhâpâni**
Italian	**Italiyâ'i**
Pakistani	**Pâkestâni**
Portuguese	**Portagâli**
Russian	**Rusi**
Scottish	**Eskâtlandi**
Spanish	**Espâniyâ'i**
Welsh	**Ahl-e Vaylz**

Where were you born?	**Shomâ kojâ be donyâ âmadid?**

I was born in ...

Man dar ... be donyâ âmadam.

—Regional nationalities

Meliyat-e eghlimi

Afghanistan	**Afghânestân**
—Afghani	**—Afghâni**
Armenia	**Armanestân**
—Armenian	**—Armani**
Azerbaijan	**Âzarbâyjân**
—Azerbaijani	**— Âzarbâyjâni**
Georgia	**Gorjestân**
—Georgian	**—Gorjestâni**
Iraq	**Arâgh**
—Iraqi	**—Arâghi**
Kirgizstan	**Kirghizestân**
—Kirgiz	**—Kirghiz**
Tajikistan	**Tâjikistân**
—Tajik	**—Tâjik**
Turkey	**Torkiye**
—Turkish	**—Tork**
Turkmenistan	**Torkamanestân**
—Turkmen	**—Torkaman**
Uzbekistan	**Ozbekistân**
—Uzbek	**—Ozbek**
Kurd	**Kord**
Baluchi	**Baluch**
Arab	**Arab**

—Occupations

Kar-ha

What do you do?

Shomâ che kâr mikonid?

I am a/an ...

Man ... hastam.

    academic   **ostâd**

    accountant   **hesâbdâr**

administrator	**mas'ul-e omur-e edâri**
agronomist	**keshâvarzi shenâs**
aid worker	**madâdkâr**
analyst	**mofaser**
architect	**me'mâr**
artist	**naghâsh**
banker	**bânkdâr**
blacksmith	**âhangar**
business person	**kâseb; tâjer**
carpenter	**najâr**
civil servant	**kârmand-e dawlat**
consultant	**moshâver**
medical	**motakhases**
dentist	**dandân pezeshk**
designer	**tarâh**
diplomat	**diplumât**
doctor	**doktur-e pezeshk**
economist	**motakhases-e eghtesâd**
engineer	**mohandes**
factory worker	**kârgar**
farmer	**keshâvarz**
film-maker	**filmsâz**
joiner	**najâr**
journalist	**khabar-negâr**
judge	**qâzi**
lawyer	**vakil**
mechanic	**mekânik**
midwife	**ghâbela**
negotiator	**miyânjigar-e mozâkerât**
nurse	**parastâr**
observer	**moshâhede konande**

office worker	**kârmand**
pediatrician	**doktôr-e atfâl**
pilot	**khalebân**
political analyst	**rizhehgar-e olum-e siyâsi**
relief worker	**kârmand-e emdâdi**
scientist	**dâneshmand**
secretary	**monshi**
soldier	**sarbâz**
specialist	**motakhases**
student	**dâneshju**
surgeon	**jarâh**
tailor	**khayât**
teacher	**mo'alem**
therapist	**terâpist**
tourist	**turist**
trader	**tâjer**
volunteer	**dâvatalab**
writer	**nevisande**

I work in ...	**Man dar ... kâr mikonam.**
advertising	**e'lânât**
an aid agency	**âzhâns-e emdâd**
a charity	**mo'asese-ye khayriye**
the hotel industry	**sanâ'ye-ye hoteldâri**
industry	**san'at**
insurance	**bime**
I.T.	**kâmpyuter**
the leisure industry	**senf-e tafrihâti**
marketing	**bâzâr yâbi**
the media	**resâne-hâ**
an office	**yek daftar**

the retail industry	**senf-e khorda forushi**
sales	**forushendagi**
a shop	**yek dôkân**
telecommunications	**mokhâberât**
tourism	**sanâ'ye-ye jehângardi**

—Age · Sen

How old are you?	**Chand sâl-etun e?**
I am ... years old.	**Man ... sâl-am e.**

—Family · Khanevade

Are you married?

said to a man:	**Shomâ zan dârid?**
said to a woman:	**Shomâ shôhar kardid/dârid?**

I am not married.

said by a man:	**Man zan nadâram.**
said by a woman:	**Man shôhar nakardam/nadâram.**

I am married.

said by a man:	**Man zan dâram.**
said by a woman:	**Man shôhar kardam/dâram.**
said by both sexes:	**Man arusi kardam.**
I am divorced.	**Man talâgh gereftam.**
I am widowed.	**Man bive hastam.**
How many children do you have?	**Chand tâ bache dârid?**
I don't have any children.	**Man bache nadâram.**
I have a daughter.	**Man yek dokhtar dâram.**
I have a son.	**Man yek pesar dâram.**

Do you have a boyfriend?	**Shomâ dust-pesar dârid?**
Do you have a girlfriend?	**Shomâ dust-dokhtar dârid?**
What is his/her name?	**Esm-esh chi ye?**
How many sisters do you have?	**Chand tâ khâhar dârid?**
How many brothers do you have?	**Chand tâ barâdar dârid?**
How many sisters and brothers do you have?	**Chand tâ khâhar-barâdar dârid?**

father		**pedar**
mother		**mâdar**
grandfather		**pedar bozorg**
grandmother		**mâdar bozorg**
granddaughter/grandson		**nave**
brother		**barâdar**
sister		**khâhar**
daughter		**dokhtar**
son		**pesar**
girl		**dokhtar**
boy		**bache**
twins		**dô-ghulu**
child		**bache**
children		**bache-hâ**
baby boy		**pesar bache**
baby girl		**dokhtar bache**
teenager		**nôjavân**
old person	*male*	**âghâ-ye mosen**
	female	**khânom-e mosen**
husband		**shôhar**
wife		**zan; khânom**
co-wife		**havu**
family		**khânavâde**

man	**mard**
woman	**zan**
person	**âdam**
people	**mardom**
orphan	**yatim**

—Religion — Din

I am (a) ...	**Man ... hastam.**
Muslim	**Mosalmân**
Buddhist	**az maz-hab-e Budâ**
Christian	**Masihi**
Catholic	**Kâtulik**
Hindu	**Hendu**
Jewish	**Yahudi**
Orthodox	**Ortodoks**
I am not religious.	**Man din nadâram.** or
	Man maz-habi nistam.

Religious heritage . . .

Iranians are Muslims, mostly Shi'ite with some Sunni communities. Neighboring Iraq has also a Shi'ite majority. Small groups of Christians (including Armenians and Assyrians), Zoroastrians, Jews, and Baha'is are also found across the country. Mosques (**masjed-hâ**) and madrasas (**madrase-hâ** — religious schools) have always played an important part in the development of the Iranian people and state, and Islam makes its presence felt through the often stunning religious buildings still standing throughout the country.

HOLIDAYS & FESTIVALS — There are a wide variety of traditional festivals celebrated in every village and region. Important dates in the national calendar are **Ramazân** (Ramadan, the month of fasting), **Id al-Fetr**, when the end of Ramadan and fasting is celebrated, and, three months later, **Id al-Haj** or **Id al-Adhâ**, which is when pilgrims traditionally celebrate their return from visiting Mecca. **Ashura** commemorates the martyrdom in 680 C.E. of Hussein, grandson of the Prophet Muhammad. Passion plays re-enacting the martyrdom are staged and many take part in mourning rituals. **Nô Ruz** is the Iranian New Year or Spring Festival (March 21st).

4. LANGUAGE

ZABAN

Do you speak Farsi?	(Âyâ) shomâ Fârsi baladid?
Do you speak English?	(Âyâ) shomâ Ingilisi baladid?
Do you speak Arabic?	(Âyâ) shomâ Arabi baladid?
Do you speak Armenian?	(Âyâ) shomâ Armani baladid?
Do you speak Azeri?	(Âyâ) shomâ Âzeri baladid?
Do you speak Chinese?	(Âyâ) shomâ Chini baladid?
Do you speak Dutch?	(Âyâ) shomâ Holandi baladid?
Do you speak French?	(Âyâ) shomâ Farânsavi baladid?
Do you speak German?	(Âyâ) shomâ Âlemâni baladid?
Do you speak Hindi?	(Âyâ) shomâ zabân-e Hendi baladid?
Do you speak Italian?	(Âyâ) shomâ Itâliyâ'i baladid?
Do you speak Kurdish?	(Âyâ) shomâ Kordi baladid?
Do you speak Russian?	(Âyâ) shomâ Rusi baladid?
Do you speak Spanish?	(Âyâ) shomâ Espâniyâ'i baladid?
Do you speak Swedish?	(Âyâ) shomâ Suedi baladid?

LANGUAGE

Do you speak Turkish?	**(Âyâ) shomâ Torki baladid?**
Do you speak Urdu?	**(Âyâ) shomâ zabân-e Ordu baladid?**
Does anyone speak English?	**Kesi hast Ingilisi balad bâshad?**
I speak a little ...	**Man yek kam ... baladam.**
I don't speak ...	**Man ... balad nistam.**
I don't know any ...	**Man hich ... balad nistam.**
I understand.	**Man mifahmam.**
I don't understand.	**Man nemifahmam.**
What does this mean?	**In che mâni dârad?**
Please point to the word in the book.	**Loghat râ dar ketâb neshân bedenid, lotfan.**
Please wait while I look up the word.	**Lotfan sabr konid tâ man loghat râ paydâ konam.**
Could you speak more slowly, please?	**Lotfan yek kam âhastetar sohbat konid.**
Could you repeat that?	**Mitavânid ân râ tekrâr konid?**
How do you say ... in Farsi?	**Be Fârsi chetur miguyid ...?**
What does ... mean?	**... che mâni dârad?**
How do you pronounce this word?	**In loghat râ chetor talafoz mikonid?**

I speak Farsi.	**Man Fârsi baladam.**
I speak English.	**Man Ingilisi baladam.**
I speak Arabic.	**Man Arabi baladam.**
I speak Armenian.	**Man Armani baladam.**
I speak Azeri.	**Man Âzeri baladam.**
I speak Chinese.	**Man Chini baladam.**
I speak Dutch.	**Man Holandi baladam.**
I speak French.	**Man Farânsavi baladam.**
I speak German.	**Man Âlemâni baladam.**
I speak Hindi.	**Man zabân-e Hendi baladam.**
I speak Italian.	**Man Itâliyâ'i baladam.**
I speak Kurdish.	**Man Kordi baladam.**
I speak Russian.	**Man Rusi baladam.**
I speak Spanish.	**Man Espâniyâ'i baladam.**
I speak Swedish.	**Man Suedi baladam.**
I speak Turkish.	**Man Torki baladam.**
I speak Urdu.	**Man zabân-e Ordu baladam.**

5. BUREAUCRACY
KAGHAZ-E EDARI

name	**esm**
surname	**esm-e fâmil**
middle name	**esm-e vasati**
address	**âdres**
date of birth	**târikh-e tavalod**
place of birth	**mahal-e tavalod**
nationality	**meliyat; tâbe'iyat**
age	**sen**
sex: male/female	**mard/zan**
religion	**din**
reason for travel:	**dalil-e safar:**
business	**tejârat**
tourism	**sayâhat; turizm**
work	**kâr**
personal	**shakhsi**
profession	**shoghl**
marital status	**vaz'iyat-e ezdevâji**
single	**mojarad**
married *male*	**mota'ahel**
female	**shôhardâr**
divorced	**talâq shode**
date	**târikh**
date of arrival	**târikh-e vorud**
date of departure	**târikh-e khoruj**
passport	**pâsport**
passport number	**shomâre-ye pâsport**
visa	**viza**
currency	**pul**

—Inquiries

Moraje'at

Is this the correct form?	**In form dorost ast?**
What does this mean?	**In che ma'ni midehad?**
Where is ...'s office?	**Daftar-e ... kojâst?**
Which floor is it on?	**Dar kodâm tabaqe hast?**
Does the lift work?	**Asânsur kâr mikonad?**
Is Mr./Mrs./Miss ... in?	**Âghâ-ye/Khânom-e ... hast?**
Please tell him/her that I am here.	**Lotfan, beheshân befarmâ'id ke man injâ hastam.**
I can't wait, I have an appointment.	**Man nemitavânam montazer bâsham, molâqât dâram.**
Tell him/her that I was here.	**Beheshân befarmâ'id ke man injâ budam.**

—Ministries

Vezarat-ha

Ministry of Defense	**Vezârat-e Defâ'**
Ministry of Agriculture	**Vezârat-e Keshâvarzi**
Ministry of Foreign Affairs	**Vezârat-e Omur-e Khâreji**
Ministry of Home Affairs	**Vezârat-e Keshvar**
Ministry of Tourism	**Vezârat-e Turizm**
Ministry of Finance	**Vezârat-e Eghtesâd**
Ministry of Health	**Vezârat-e Behdâsht**
Ministry of Education	**Vezârat-e Âmuzesh va Parvaresh**
Ministry of Justice	**Vezârat-e Dâdgostari**
Ministry of Commerce and Industry	**Vezârat-e Tejârat ve Sanâye**
Ministry of Information	**Vezârat-e Etelâ'ât**
Ministry of Culture	**Vezârat-e Farhang**

6. TRAVEL

SAFAR

> **PUBLIC TRANSPORT** — Buses can be too crammed for comfort. Far more practical are taxis or private cars hailed in the street or the minibuses that stop at pre-determined pickup points. You pay the driver or his assistant as you get out. Rail travel is slow, subject to long delays mid-journey and less safe than by road. Bicycles and motorbikes are not difficult to find but practically are not much use outside of the town spaces in view of Iran's huge expanse and vastly different terrains.

What time does the ...	**Sâ'at chand ...**
airplane leave/arrive?	**havâpêmâ harekat mikonad/miresad?**
boat leave/arrive?	**kashti harekat mikonad/miresad?**
bus leave/arrive?	**otobus harekat mikonad/miresad?**
train leave/arrive?	**ghatâr harekat mikonad/miresad?**
minibus leave/arrive?	**minibus harekat mikonad/miresad?**
The plane is delayed.	**Havâpemâ ta'khir dârad.**
The plane is cancelled.	**Havâpemâ kânsel shode.**
The train is delayed.	**Qatâr ta'khir dârad.**
The train is cancelled.	**Qatâr kânsel shode.**
How long will it be delayed?	**Cheqadr ta'khir dârad?**

There is a delay of ... minutes.	**... daghighe ta'khir dârad.**
There is a delay of ... hours.	**... sâ'at ta'khir dârad.**

—Buying tickets

Excuse me, where is the ticket office?	**Bebakhshid, gishe-ye bilit kojâ-st?**
Where can I buy a ticket?	**Kojâ mitunam bilit bekharam?**
I want to go to ...	**Man mikhâm be ... beravam/beram.**
I want a ticket to ...	**Man yek bilit be ... mikhâm.**
I would like ...	**Man ... mikhâm.**
a one-way ticket	**bilit-e yek tarafe**
a return ticket	**bilit-e raft o bar gasht**
Do I pay in riyals or in dollars?	**Bâ riyâl bepardâzam yâ bâ dolâr?**
You must pay in riyals.	**Bâyad bâ riyâl bepardâzid.**
You must pay in dollars.	**Bâ dolâr bâyad bepardâzid.**
You can pay in either.	**Bâ har kodâm mitavânid bepardâzid.**
Can I reserve a place?	**Yek jâ mitavânam rezerv konam?**
How long does the trip take?	**In safar cheghadr tul mikeshad?**
Is it a direct route?	**Mostaghim miravad?**

—Air

Hava

Is there a flight to ... ?	**Be ... parvâz hast?**
When is the next flight to ... ?	**Parvâz-e ba'di be ... kay hast?**
How long is the flight?	**In parvâz cheghadr tul mikeshad?**
What is the flight number?	**Shomâre-ye parvâz chi hast?**
You must check in at ...	**Shomâ bâyad dam-e ... chek-in konid.**
Is the flight delayed?	**Parvâz ta'khir dârad?**
How many hours is the flight delayed?	**Parvâz chand sâ'at ta'khir dârad?**
Is this the flight for ... ?	**In parvâz-e ... hast?**
Is that the flight from ... ?	**Ân parvâz az ... miyâyad?**
When is the Paris flight arriving?	**Parvâz-e Pâris kay miresad?**
Is it on time?	**Sar-e vaqt miresad?**
Is it late?	**Dir miresad?**
Do I have to change planes?	**Man havâpayma bâyad avaz konam?**
Has the plane left Paris yet?	**Havâpayma az Pâris harekat karde?**
What time does the plane take off?	**Havâpayma sâ'at chand parvâz mikonad?**
What time do we arrive in Teheran?	**Sâ'at chand be Tehrân miresim?**
I wish to confirm my flight.	**Man mikhâham parvâzam râ kânfarm konam.**
excess baggage	**bâr-e ezâfe**
international flight	**parvâz-e baynolmelali**
national/internal flight	**parvâz-e dâkheli**

— Bus

Otobus

bus stop/bus station	**istgâh-e otobus**
Where is the bus stop?	**Istgâh-e otobus kojâ-st?**
Which bus goes to ... ?	**Kodâm otobus ba ... miravad?**
Please take me to the bus station.	**Lotfan marâ be istgâh-e otobus bebarid.**
Where can I get a bus to ... ?	**Otobus be ... az kojâ mitunam begiram?**
Which bus goes to ... ?	**Kodâm otobus be ... miravid?**
Does this bus go to ... ?	**In otobus be ... miravad?**
How often do buses pass by?	**Otobus-hâ az injâ chand vaght be chand vaght miravand?**
What time is the ... bus?	**Otobus-e ... sâ'at chand miyâyad?**
first	**aval**
next	**ba'di**
last	**âkhari**
When is the first bus to ... ?	**Avalin otobus be ... sâ'at chand ast?**
When is the next bus to ... ?	**Otobus-e ba'di be ... sâ'at chand ast.**
When is the last bus to ... ?	**Âkharin otobus be ... sâ'at chand ast.**
Do I have to change buses?	**Otobus bâyad avaz konam?**
How long is the journey?	**Safar cheghadr tul mikeshad?**
What is the fare?	**Bilet cheghadr ast?**
Will you let me know when we get to ... ?	**Vaghti ke be ... residim be man miguyid?**

I want to get off at ...	**Mikham dar ... piyâde shavam.**
Stop, I want to get off!	**Negah dârid, mikhâm piyâde shavam!**
Please let me off at the next stop.	**Lotfan marâ dam-e istgâh-e ba'di piyâde konid.**
Please let me off here.	**Lotfan injâ marâ piyâde konid.**
I need my luggage, please.	**Bâram râ mikhâm, lotfan.**
That's my bag.	**Ân sâk-e man hast.**

—By rail

Rah ahan

Please take me to the railway station.	**Lotfan marâ be istgâh-e ghatâr bebarid.**
Is there a timetable?	**Âyâ jadval-e safar hast?**
Where can I buy tickets?	**Kojâ mitavânam bilit bekharam?**
The train leaves from platform ...	**Ghatâr az saku-ye ... harekat mikonad.**
Which platform should I go to?	**Be kodâm saku beram?**
platform one	**saku shomâre yek**
platform two	**saku shomâre dô**
Is this the right platform for ... ?	**In saku barâye ... dorost ast?**
You must change trains at ...	**Dar ... bâyad ghatâr avaz konid.**
Passengers must ...	**Mosâferân bâyad ...**
change trains.	**ghatâr avaz konand.**
change platforms.	**saku avaz konand.**
Will the train leave on time?	**In ghatâr sar-e vaght? harekat mikonad?**

| There will be a delay of ... minutes. | **... daghighe ta'khir khâhad bud.** |
| There will be a delay of ... hours. | **... sâ'at ta'khir khâhad bud.** |

—Taxi

Taxi!	**Tâksi!**
Where can I get a taxi?	**Kojâ mitavânam tâksi begiram?**
Please could you get me a taxi.	**Lotfan barâye man tâksi begerid?**
Can you take me to ... ?	**Marâ be ... mitavânid bebarid?**
Please take me to ...	**Lotfan marâ be ... bebarid.**
How much will it cost to ... ?	**Tâ ... cheghadr mishavad?**
How much?	**Cheghadr?**
To this address, please.	**Be in âdres, lotfan.**
Turn left.	**Dast-e chap bepichid.**
Turn right.	**Dast-e râst bepichid.**
Go straight ahead.	**Mostaghim beravid.**
Stop!	**Negah dârid!**
Don't stop!	**Negah nadârid!**
I'm in a hurry.	**Man ajale dâram.**
Please drive more slowly!	**Lotfan yavâshtar rânandegi konid!**
Here is fine, thank you.	**Injâ khob ast, tashakor.**
The next corner, please.	**Nabsh-e ba'di, lotfan.**
The next street to the left.	**Kuche-ye ba'di, dast-e chap.**
The next street to the right.	**Kuche-ye ba'di, dast-e râst.**
Stop here!	**Injâ negah dârid!**

Stop the car, I want to get out.	**Mâshin râ negah dârid,mikhâm piyâde beshavam.**
Please wait for me here.	**Lotfan injâ montazer-e bâshid.**
Please take me to the airport.	**Marâ be forudgâh bebarid.**

—General phrases

I want to get off at ...	**Mikhâm dam-e ... piyâde beshavam.**
Excuse me!	**Bebakhshid!**
Excuse me, may I get by?	**Mibakhshid, momken ast rad shavam.**
I want to get out (of the bus/taxi).	**Mikhâm (az otobus/ tâksi) piyâde beshavam.**
These are my bags.	**Inhâ sâk-hâ-ye-man hastand.**
Please put them there.	**Lotfan injâ begozârid.**
Is this seat free?	**In jâ khâli ast?**
I think that's my seat.	**Fekr mikonam ân jâ-ye-man bâshad.**
I need my luggage, please.	**Bâr-am râ mikhâham, lotfan.**

—Travel words

Kalemat-e safar

airport	**forudgâh**
airport tax	**mâliyât-e forudgâh**
ambulance	**âmbulâns**
arrivals	**vorud**
bag(s)	**sâk(-hâ)**
baggage	**bâr**

baggage counter	**qesmat-e bâr**
bicycle	**dô-charkhe**
boarding pass	**kârt-e savâr shodan**
boat	**ghâyegh**
border	**marz**
bus stop	**istgâh-e otobus**
camel	**shotor**
car	**mâshin**
carriage *horse-drawn*	**gâri**
check-in	**chek-in**
check-in counter	**miz-e chek-in**
closed	**baste**
customs	**gomrok**
delay	**ta'khir**
departures	**khoruj**
dining car *of train*	**bufe**
emergency exit	**khoruj-e ezterâri**
entrance	**vorudi**
exit	**khoruj**
express	**sari'-us-sayr**
ferry	**keshti**
foot: on foot	**piyâde**
4-wheel drive	**jip**
frontier	**marz**
helicopter	**helikopter**
horse	**asb**
horse and cart	**asb ve gâri**
information	**etelâ'ât**
ladies/gents toilets	**tuvâlet-e zanâne/**
	tuvâlet-e mardâne
local	**mahali**
lorry/truck	**kâmyon; terayli**
luggage	**bâr**
metro/subway	**(tunel-e) zir zamin;**
	metro

motorbike	**motor**
mule	**ghâter**
no entry	**vorud mamnu' (ast)**
no smoking	**sigâr keshidan mamnu' ast**
open	**bâz**
path	**râh**
platform	**saku**
platform number	**shomâre-ye saku**
railway	**râh âhan**
reserved	**rezerv shode**
radio taxi	**tâksi telefôni**
road	**jâde**
tarmac road	**jâde-ye âsfâlt**
sign	**neshâni**
sleeping car *of train*	**vâgon-e takhtkhâbdâr**
station	**istgâh**
bus station	**istgâh-e otobus**
train station	**istgâh-e ghatâr**
subway/metro	**(tunel-e) zir zamin; metro**
telephone	**telefôn**
ticket office	**edâre-ye forush-e bilit**
timetable	**jadval-e safar**
toilet(s)	**tuvâlet(-hâ)**
town center	**markaz-e shahr**
train station	**istgâh-e ghatâr**
truck/lorry	**kâmyon; terayli**
van	**vânet**

7. ACCOMMODATION
EGHAMATGAH

I am looking for a ...	**Man donbâl-e ... migardam.**
hotel	**hotel**
guesthouse	**pânsyôn**
hostel	**hostel**
Is there anywhere I can stay for the night?	**Jâ'i hast ke man mitavânam shab bemânam?**
Is there anywhere we can stay for the night?	**Jâ'i hast ke mâ mitavânim shab bemânim?**
Where is ... ?	**... kojâ-st?**
a cheap hotel	**yek hotel-e arzân**
a good hotel	**yek hotel-e khob**
a nearby hotel	**yek hotel-e nazdik**
a clean hotel	**yek hotel-e tamiz**
What is the address?	**Âdres-esh kojâ-st?**
Could you write the address please?	**Âdres râ mitavânid benevisid?**

—At the hotel

Dar hotel

Do you have any rooms free?	**Otâgh-e khâli dârid?**
I would like ...	**Man ... mikhâham.**
a single room	**yek otâgh-e yek nafari**
a double room	**yek otâgh-e dô nafari**
We'd like a room.	**Mâ yek otâgh mikhâhim.**

We'd like two rooms.	**Mâ dô tâ otâgh mikhâhim.**
I want a room with ...	**Man yek otâgh bâ ... mikhâham.**
a bathroom	**hamâm**
a shower	**dush**
a television	**televizyon**
a window	**panjere**
a double bed	**takht-e dô nafari**
a balcony	**balkon**
a view	**manzare**
I want a room that's quiet.	**Man yek otâgh-e ârâm mikhâham.**

—Booking in

How long will you be staying?	**Barâye che modat mimânid?**
How many nights?	**Chand shab?**
I'm going to stay for ...	**Man barâye ... mimânam.**
one day	**yek ruz**
two days	**dô ruz**
one week	**yek hafte**
Do you have any I.D./a passport?	**Shenâshnâme/Pâsport dârid?**
Sorry, we're full.	**Bebakhshid, jâ nadârim.**
I have a reservation.	**Man ghablan otâgh rezerv kardam.**
Is the room ready?	**Âyâ otâgh hâzer e?**
My name is ...	**Esm-e man ... hast.**
May I speak to the manager please?	**Momken ast bâ modir sohbat konam.**
I have to meet someone here.	**Injâ bâ kesi molâghât dâram.**

How much is it per night?	**Shabi cheghadr mishavad?**
How much is it per week?	**Barâye yek hafte cheghadr mishavad?**
How much is it per person?	**Nafari cheghadr mishavad?**
It's ... per day.	**Ruzi ... mishavad.**
It's ... per week.	**Hafte'i ... mishavad.**
It's ... per person.	**Nafari ... mishavad.**

—Choosing a room

Can I see the room?	**Otâgh râ mishe did?**
Are there any other rooms?	**Bâz ham otâgh hast?**
Is there ... ?	**... hast?**
airconditioning	**kuler**
a telephone	**telefôn**
hot water	**âb-e garm**
laundry service	**servis-e khoshu'i**
room service	**servis-e otâgh**
It's fine, I'll take it.	**Khob ast, in râ migeram.**
No, I don't like it.	**Nah, khosham nemiyâyad.**
It's too ...	**Khayli ... ast.**
cold	**sard**
hot	**garm**
big	**bozorg**
dark	**târik**
small	**kuchek**
dirty	**kasif**
It's too noisy.	**Khayli sedâ miyâyad.**
Where is the bathroom?	**Hamâm kojâ-st?**

Is there hot water all day?	**Tamâm-e ruz âb-e garm hast?**
Do you have a safe?	**Sandoq-e amniyat dârid?**
Is there anywhere to wash clothes?	**Jâ'i hast barâye shostan-e lebâs?**
Can I use the telephone?	**Telefôn râ mitavânam estefâde konam?**
Can I have the key to my room?	**Kelid-e otâgham râ be man midehid?**

—Needs

Ehtiyajat-ha

I need ...	**Man ... ehityâjat dâram.**
candles	**sham'**
toilet paper	**dastmâl tuvâlet**
soap	**sâbun**
clean sheets	**malâfe-ye tamiz**
an extra blanket	**yek patu-ye ezâfe**
drinking water	**âb khordan**
a heater	**yek bukhâri**
a lightbulb	**yek lâmp**
a mosquito net	**pashakhâne**
insect repellant	**davâ-ye pashe**

Please change the sheets.	**Lotfan, malâfe-hâ râ avaz konid.**
I can't open the window.	**Panjare râ nemitavânam bâz konam.**
I can't close the window.	**Panjare râ nemitavânam bebandam.**
I have lost my key.	**Kelidam râ gom kardam.**
Do you have a needle and thread?	**Suzan nakh dârid?**

The shower won't work.	**Dush kâr nemikonad.**
How do I get hot water?	**Az kojâ âb-e garm begiram?**
The water has been cut off.	**Âb ghat' shod.**
The electricity has been cut off.	**Bargh ghat' shod.**
The gas has run out.	**Gâz ghat' shod.**
The airconditioning doesn't work.	**Kuler kâr nemikonad.**
The heating doesn't work.	**Shôfâzh ghat' shod.**
The heater doesn't work.	**Bukhâri kâr nemikonad.**
The phone doesn't work.	**Telefôn kâr nemikonad.**
The toilet won't flush.	**Tuvâlet flâsh-esh kharâb e.**
The toilet is blocked.	**Tuvâlet gerefte shode.**
I can't switch off the tap.	**Shir râ nemitavânam bebandam.**
I can't close the window.	**Penjere baste nemishavad.**
I can't lock the door.	**Dar ghofl nemishavad.**
I need a plug for the bath.	**Barâye vân yek plâg lâzem-e.**
Where is the plug socket?	**Sâket-e dô shâkhe kojâ-st?**
There's a strange insect in my room.	**Yek hashare-ye ajib dar otâgh-e man ast.**
There's an animal in my room.	**Yek hayvân dar otâgh-e man ast.**

—Leaving
Raftan

wake-up call	**zang-e bidâr shodan**
Could you please wake me up at ... o'clock?	**Lotfan marâ sâ'at-e ... bidâr konid.**
I am leaving now.	**Hâlâ man miravam.**
We are leaving now.	**Hâlâ mâ miravim.**
May I pay the bill now?	**Hâlâ hesâb râ mitavânam bedeham?**

—Hotel words
Loghat-he-ye hotel

bathroom	**hamâm**
bed	**takht**
blanket	**patu**
candle	**sham'**
candles	**sham'-hâ**
ceiling	**saghf**
chair	**sandali**
cold water	**âb-e sard**
cupboard	**ghafase**
doorlock	**qofl-e dâr**
electricity	**bargh**
excluded	**shâmel nashode**
extra	**ezâfe**
floor *story*	**tabaghe**
fridge	**yakhchâl**
hot water	**âb-e garm**
included	**shâmel; shâmel shode**
key	**kelid**
lamp	**cherâgh**
laundry	**khoshk-shu'i**
light *electric*	**cherâgh**
mattress	**toshak**
meal	**ghazâ**
meals	**ghazâ-hâ**

mirror	**âyene**
name	**esm; nâm**
noisy	**por-e sarsedâ**
padlock	**ghofl**
pillow	**bâlesht**
(bath) plug	**plâg**
(electric) plug	**dô shâkhe**
quiet	**sâket**
roof	**bâm**
room	**otâgh**
room number	**shomâre-ye otâgh**
sheet	**malâfe**
shelf	**tâghche**
shower	**dush**
stairs	**pele**
suitcase	**chamedân**
surname	**nâm-e khândevâdegi**
table	**miz**
towel	**hôle**
veranda	**terâs**
wall	**divâr**
water	**âb**
window	**panjere**

8. FOOD & DRINK
GHAZA VE NUSHIDANI

Food plays an important part of Iranian life for Iranians all over the world, and important events in all aspects of life and the year are marked with a feast of one form or another. Food is a very important part of Iranian hospitality — it is both the host's duty to make sure his or her guests are eating and it is the guest's duty to partake of what is offered. **Polav** is king in Iranian cuisine, and new guests are traditionally fed this dish above all others. Every Iranian home will offer you a dazzling variety of dishes, delicacies and drinks, which vary from area to area and from season to season.

breakfast	**sobhâne**
lunch	**nâhâr**
dinner; supper	**shâm**
I'm hungry.	**Man gorosname.** *or* **Man gorosne hastam.**
I'm thirsty.	**Man teshname.** *or* **Man teshne hastam.**
Have you eaten yet?	**Shomâ ghazâ khordid?**
Do you know a good restaurant?	**Rasturân-e khob mishenâsid?**

—At the restaurant
Dar rasturan

Do you have a table, please?	**Yek miz dârid, lotfan?**
I would like a table for ... people, please.	**Man yek miz barâye ... nafar mikhâham, lotfan.**
Can I see the menu please?	**Menyu râ mitavânam bebinam, lotfan?**

FOOD & DRINK

I'm still looking at the menu.	**Hanuz dâram menyu râ negâh mikonam.**
I would like to order. now.	**Mikhâstam al'ân sefâresh konam.**
What's this?	**In chi hast?** *or* **In chi-ye?**
Is it spicy? *(hot)*	**Tond ast?**
Does it have meat in it?	**Âyâ in gusht dârad?**
Do you have ... ?	**... dârid?**
We don't have ...	**Mâ ... nadârim.**
What would you recommend?	**Shomâ che tavsiye mikonid?**
Do you want ... ?	**... mikhâhid?**
Can I order some more ... ?	**Mishavad/Mishe baz ham az ... sefâresh konam?**
That's all, thank you.	**Hamin, motashakeram.**
That's enough, thanks.	**Kafi ast, mersi.**
I haven't finished yet.	**Hanuz tamâm nakardam.**
I have finished eating.	**Ghazâ râ tamâm kardam.**
I am full up!	**Man sir shodam!**
Where are the toilets?	**Dast-shu'i kojâ-st?**
I am a vegetarian.	**Man giyah-khur-am.**
I don't eat meat.	**Man gusht nemikhoram.**
I don't eat chicken or fish.	**Man morgh yâ mâhi nemikhoram.**
I don't eat nuts.	**Man bâdâm nemikhoram.**
I don't smoke.	**Man sigâr nemikesham.**

FOOD & DRINK

(I don't drink alcohol. **Man mashrub nemikhoram.**)

Note that alcohol is not permitted in Iran.

—Needs

I would like ...	**Man ... mikhâstam.**
an ashtray	**zir sigâri**
the menu	**menyu**
the bill	**hesâb râ**
a glass of water	**yek livân âb**
another glass	**yek livân-e digar**
a bottle of water	**yek shishe âb**
another bottle	**yek shishe-ye digar**
a bottle-opener	**dar bâz-kon**
a corkscrew	**dar bâz-kon**
a drink	**(yek) nushidani**
a chair	**(yek) sandali**
another plate	**yek boshghâb-e digar**
a napkin	**(yek) dastmâl**
a glass	**(yek) livân**
a tea-glass	**(yek) estekân**
a cup	**(yek) fenjân**
another cup	**yek fenjân-e digar**
a knife	**(yek) kârd/châqu**
a fork	**(yek) changâl**
a plate	**(yek) boshqâb**
a bowl	**(yek) kâse**
a jug	**(yek) pârch**
a spoon	**(yek) ghâshogh**
a table	**(yek) miz**
a teaspoon	**(yek) ghâshogh chây khuri**
a toothpick	**(yek) khalâl dandân**
a sugarlump	**ghand**

too much	**ziyâd**
too little	**kam**
not enough	**kam**
empty	**khâli**
full	**por**

—Tastes — Cheshayi-ha

fresh	**tâze**
raw	**khâm**
uncooked	**nâpokhte**
cooked	**pokhte**
ripe	**reside**
tender	**narm**
tough *meat*	**seft**
spicy (hot)	**tond**
stale	**mânde**
bread	**bayât**
sour	**torsh**
sweet	**shirin**
bitter	**talkh**
hot	**garm; dâgh**
cold	**sard**
salty	**shur**
tasteless	**bi maze**
bad; spoiled	**kharâb**
tasty	**khosh maze**
good	**khob**

—General food words — Loghat-ha-ye omumi baraye ghaza

bread	**nân**
burger	**berger**
butter	**kare**
cake	**kayki shirini**

candy	**âb nabât**
caviar	**khâvyâr**
cheese	**panir**
chewing gum	**âdâms**
coriander	**gishniz**
dessert	**deser**
egg	**tokhm-e morgh**
boiled egg	**tokhm-e âb paz**
fat	**charbi**
flour	**ârd**
french fries	**sib zamini sorkh karde**
garlic	**sir**
ghee	**rôghan**
ginger	**zenjebil**
gravy	**âb-e gusht**
honey	**asal**
ice-cream	**bastani**
jam; jelly	**morabâ**
ketchup	**sôs**
loaf	**nân-e sândvich**
margarine	**marjarin**
meat	**gusht**
menu	**menyu**
mint	**na'nâ**
mustard	**khardal**
nut: almond	**bâdâm**
pistachio	**peste**
walnut	**gerdu**
oil	**rôghan**
pasta	**mâkâroni**
pepper	**felfel**
pickles	**torshi**
pizza	**pitsa**
provisions	**ghazâ**

rice:	uncooked	**berenj**
	cooked	**polav**
salad		**sâlâd**
salt		**namak**
sandwich		**sândvich**
sauce		**sôs**
shopping		**kharid**
soup		**sup**
spice		**adviye**
sugar		**shekar**
syrup		**sharbat**
	treacle	**shire**
table		**miz**
tablecloth	table	**rumizi**
	floor	**sofre**
teapot		**ghuri**
tray		**sini**
vinegar		**serke**
yogurt		**mâst**

RICE — Berenj is uncooked rice. All cooked rice in Farsi cuisine becomes pilau (**polav**) or some other term depending on the dish. Plain white rice is known as **chelav**.

—Vegetables   Sabzijat

aubergine; eggplant	**bâdemjân**
beans	**lubiyâ**
beetroot	**choghondar**
cabbage	**kalam**
carrots	**havich**
cauliflower	**gol kalam**
chickpeas	**nokhod**
corn	**javâri**
corn-on-the-cob	**balâl**
sweetcorn	**zurat**

cucumber	**khiyâr**
fennel	**raziyâne**
garlic	**sir**
lentils	**adas**
lettuce	**kâhu**
millet	**arzan**
mushroom	**qârch**
okra; lady's fingers	**bâmiye**
olives	**zaytun**
onion/onions	**piyâz**
peas	**nokhod sabz**
pepper	**felfel**
(sweet) pepper(s)	**felfel dolmeyi**
potato/potatoes	**sib zamini**
sweet potato(s)	**kachâlu**
pumpkin	**kadu tanbel**
radish	**torobche**
salad	**sâlâd**
spinach	**esfenâj**
tomato	**gôje farangi**
turnip	**shalgham**
vegetables	**sabzijât**

—Fruit & nuts   Mive o badam

almond	**bâdâm**
apple	**sib**
apricot	**zardâlu**
banana(s)	**moz**
cherry	**gilâs**
morello cherry	**âlbâlu**
dates(s)	**khormâ**
fig	**anjir**
fruit	**mive**
grape(s)	**angur**
grapefruit	**gerepfrut**

FOOD & DRINK

lemon	**limu**
lime	**limu sabz**
mango	**mângô**
melon	**kharboze**
cantelope melon	**tâlebi**
watermelon	**hendevâne**
mulberry	**tut**
nectarine	**shalil**
orange	**portoghâl**
peach	**holu**
peanuts	**bâdâm-e zamini**
pear	**golâbi**
pistachio	**peste**
plum	**âlu**
pomegranate	**anâr**
raisins	**keshmesh**
strawberries	**tut farangi**

—Meat & fish — Gusht o mahi

beef	**gusht-e gâv**
chicken	**morgh**
fish	**mâhi**
goat meat	**gusht-e boz**
kebab	**kabâb**
lamb	**gusht-e bare**
mutton	**gusht-e gusfand**
sausage	**sôsis**

CULTURAL NOTE — In Iran you will not be offered pork (**gusht-e khuk**) since it is an Islamic country. For reference purposes, "I don't eat pork" is **Man gusht-e khuk ne-mikhoram.**

—Drinks — Nushidani-ha

bottle	**shishe**
can	**ghuti**

coffee	**ghahve**
coffee with milk	**ghahve bâ shir**
cup	**fenjân**
drink; a cool drink	**nushâbe**
fruit juice	**âb mive**
glass	**gelâs**
ice	**yakh**
with ice	**bâ yakh**
no ice	**bedun-e yakh**
lemon squash	**sharbat-e limu**
milk	**shir**
mineral water	**âb-e ma'dani**
saucer	**na'lbaki**
tea	**chây**
tea with lemon	**chây bâ limu**
tea with milk	**chây bâ shir**
tea without milk	**chây bidun-e shir**
green tea	**chây sabz**
no sugar, please!	**bidun-e shekar, lotfan!**
herbal tea	**chây giyâhi**
tea-glass	**estekân**
water	**âb**
wine	**sharâb**

CULTURAL NOTE — In Iran alcohol is not permitted for religious and legal reasons. For reference purposes, "alcohol" is **mashrub**, "wine" is **sharâb**, "beer" is **âb-e jô**, and "brandy" is **konyâk**.

FOOD & DRINK

More on food & drink . . .

The traditional diet of most Iranians consists of a dazzling range of rice, vegetables and meat, always accompanied by bread (**nân**). Herbs, soups, yogurts (**mâst**), white cheese (**panir**) and fruit add to the range, as do tea (brewed in great samovars [**samovâr**]) and home-made fruit squashes (**sharbat**). Each part of Iran has its unique cuisine based on local produce and varying herbs and spices. Some of the most popular dishes include:

Polav — rice with lamb or chicken or vegetables.

Zereshk polav — rice with barberries, chicken and saffron.

Chelô kabâb — white rice with lamb kebab (the principal dish in all Iranian restaurants).

Kabâb kubide — minced meat kebab.

Kabâb barg — pounded lean meat kebab.

Juje kabâb — poussin kebab.

Baghali polav — rice with broad beans, dill and lamb or chicken.

Sabzi polav mâhi — rice with gren herbs and fish, always eaten on New Year's Day (**Nôruz**, March 21st).

Âbghôsht   winter stew made with lamb, chick peas and tomato.

Khoresht — traditional lamb casserole, e.g.

> **Khoresht-e ghorme sabzi** — lamb with green herbs including fenugreek.

> **Khoresht-e badenjân** — with eggplants.

> **Khoresht-e ghayme** — with yellow split peas and tomato.

Âsh — thick hot winter broth, e.g. **âsh-e reshte**, made with noodles, beans and dried and whey (**kashk**).

Kuku — a kind of thick egg omelette similar to Spanish omelette, e.g. **kuku sabzi**, with green herbs, and **kuku badenjân**, with eggplants.

Dolme — stuffed vegetables, including sweet peppers, aubergines and courgettes.

Accompanying the above will be fresh herbs of the season (**sabzi khordan**) such as mint, radish, basil and spring onion, yogurt with spinach or cucumber, or salad. Finish off your meal with **baklava**, **zulbiye-bamiye** (sweets made with batter, deep-fried and soaked in syrup), ice-cream or fruit, all washed down with ubiquitous Iranian **chây** (tea).

9. DIRECTIONS
RAHNAMA'I-HA

Where is ... ?	**... kojâ-st?**
the academy	**akâdemi**
the airport	**forudgâh**
the art gallery	**gâleri-ye honar-hâ-ye zibâ**
a bank	**bânk**
the church	**kelisâ**
the city center	**markaz-e shahr**
the consulate	**konsulgari**
the embassy	**sefârat**
the ... embassy	**sefârat-e ...**
the faculty	**fâkulti**
the ... faculty	**fâkulti-ye ...**
hotel	**hotel**
the ... hotel	**hotel-e ...**
the information office	**daftar-e etelâ'ât**
the main square	**maydân-e asli**
the market	**bâzâr**
the ministry	**vezârat**
the ministry of ...	**vezârat-e ...**
the mosque	**masjed**
the Friday mosque	**masjed-e Jom'e**
the museum	**muze**
parliament	**majles**
the police station	**istgâh-e polis** *or* **kalântari**
the post office	**postkhâne**
the railway station	**istgâh-e ghatâr**
the telephone center	**markaz-e mokhâberât**

the toilets/bathroom	**tuvâlet-hâ**
the university	**dâneshgâh**
What ... is this?	**In kodâm ... ast?**
bridge	**pol**
building	**sâkhtemân**
city	**shahr**
district *in town*	**rob'**
district *in province*	**mantaghe**
river	**rudkhâne**
road	**khiyâbân**
sidestreet	**kuche**
street	**khiyâbân**
suburb	**shahrak**
town	**shahr**
village	**deh**
What is this building?	**In che sâkhtemân ist?**
What is that building?	**Ân che sâkhtemân ist?**
What time does it open?	**Sâ'at chand bâz mishavad?**
What time does it close?	**Sâ'at chand mibandad?**

—Getting there

Can I park here?	**Injâ mishe pârk konam?**
Are we on the right road for ... ?	**In râh-e ... ast?**
How many kilometers is it to ... ?	**Tâ ... chand kilometr hast?**
It is ... kilometers away.	**... kilometr fâsele dârad.**
How far is the next village?	**Deh-e ba'di cheghadr dur ast?**
Where can I find this address?	**In âdres-râ kojâ mitavânam paydâ konam?**

DIRECTIONS

Can you show me on the map?	**Ru-ye naghshe mitavânid neshân bedehid?**
How do I get to ... ?	**Chetur mitavânam be ... beravam?**
I want to go to ...	**Mikhâham be ... beravam.**
Can I walk there?	**Tâ ânjâ mitavânam piyâde beravam?**
Is it far?	**Dur ast?**
Is it near?	**Nazdik ast?**
Is it far from here?	**Az injâ dur ast?**
Is it near here?	**Be injâ nazdik ast?**
It is not far.	**Dur nist.**
Go straight ahead.	**Mostaghim beravid.**
Turn left.	**Dast-e chap bepichid.**
Turn right.	**Dast-e râst bepichid.**
to the left	**be dast-e chap**
to the right	**be dast-e râst**
to one side	**be yek taraf**
at the next corner	**dam-e gushe-ye ba'di** *or* **dam-e nabsh-e ba'di**
at the traffic lights	**dam-e cheragh ghermez**
behind	**posht**
far	**dur**
in front of	**jelô**
left	**chap**
near	**nazdik**
on	**ru**
opposite	**ru-be-ru**
outside	**birun**

right	**râst**
straight on	**mostaghim**
under	**zir**
bridge	**pol**
corner	**gushe; nabsh**
crossroads	**chahâr-râh**
one-way street	**khiyâbân-e yek tarafe**
roundabout	**maydân**
north	**shomâl**
south	**jonub**
east	**shargh**
west	**gharb**

More on thank you . . .

There are several ways to say "thank you" in Farsi, a language in which etiquette is very important and poetic phrases abound. For example: **mersi!** (the most basic form), **khayli mamnun!**, **motashakeram!**, **dast-e shomâ dard nekonad!** (= "may your hand not ache!" — used when someone has done something for you, or given you a present, to which your response is **sar-e shomâ dard nekonad!** "may your head not ache!"), **khodetun gol hastid!** (= "you are a flower yourself!", said when someone brings you flowers), **ghorbân-e shomâl/ ghorbânetun!/ ghorbân-e shomâ beram!** (= "[may I go as] your sacrifice", when you wish to express appreciation for an offer, compliment, or expression of affection). A combination of several of the above is also common, e.g. **mersi, khayli mamnun!** or **khayli mamnun, motashakeram!** are often heard.

10. SHOPPING
KHARIDAN

Where can I find a ... ?	**Kojâ mitavânam yek ... paydâ konam?**
Where can I buy ... ?	**Kojâ mitavânam ... bekharam?**
Where's the market?	**Bâzâr kojâ-st?**
Where's the nearest ... ?	**Nazdiktarin ... kojâ-st?**
Can you help me?	**Shomâ mitavânid marâ komak konid?**
Can I help you?	**Shomâ râ mitavânam komak konam?**
I'm just looking.	**Faghat negâh mikonam.**
I'd like to buy ...	**Mikhâstam ... bekharam.**
Could you show me some ... ?	**Chand tâ ... be man mitavânid neshân bedehid?**
Can I look at it?	**Mitunam bebinam-esh?**
Do you have any ... ?	**... dârid?**
This.	**In.**
That.	**Ân.**
These.	**Inhâ.**
Those.	**Ânhâ.**
I don't like it.	**(Az ash) khosham nemiyâyad.**
I like it.	**Khosham miyâyad.**
Do you have anything cheaper?	**Chizi-ye arzântar dârid?**
Do you have anything better?	**Chizi-ye behtar dârid?**
larger/smaller	**bozorgtar/kuchektar**

Do you have anything else?	**Chiz-e digari dârid?**
Do you have any others?	**Bâz ham dârid?**
Sorry, this is the only one.	**Mibakhshid, faqat in yeki râ dârim.**
I'll take it.	**Man varesh midâram.**
How much/many do you want?	**Cheghadr/chand tâ mikhâhid?**
How much is it?	**Chand ast?**
Can you write down the price?	**Ghaymat-râ mitavânid benevisid?**
Could you lower the price?	**Ghaymat-râ mita-vânid kam konid?**
I don't have much money.	**Man ziyad pul nadâram.**
Do you take credit cards?	**Kârt-e e'tebâri qabul mikonid?**
Would you like it wrapped?	**Mikhâhid bepichânamesh?**
Will that be all?	**Chiz-e digar hast?**
Thank you, good-bye.	**Motashakeram, khodâ hâfez.**
I want to return this.	**In râ mikhâham pas bedeham.**

—Outlets
Forushgah-ha

baker's	**nânvâ'i**
bank	**bânk**
barber's	**salmâni**
I'd like a haircut please.	**Lotfan muhâm-râ bezanid.**
bazaar	**bazâr**
bookshop/bookstore	**ketâb-forushi**
butcher's shop	**ghasâbi**
chemist's/pharmacy	**dârukhâne**

clothes shop	**lebâs-forushi**
dairy	**labaniyât**
dentist's surgery	**dandân-sâz**
department store	**forushgâh**
dressmaker	**khayât**
electrical goods store	**forushgâh-e lavâzem-e elektriki**
fabric shop	**pârche-forushi**
florist	**gol-forush**
greengrocer	**sabzi forush**
hairdresser	**salmâni**
hardware store	**khorde forushi**
hospital	**bimârestân**
kiosk	**kyosk**
laundry	**khoshk-shu'i**
market	**bâzâr**
newsstand	**kyosk-e ruznâme**
shoeshop	**kafsh forushi**
shop/store	**maghâze; dokân**
souvenir shop	**soghât forushi**
stationer's	**forushgâh-e lavâzem-e tahrir**
supermarket	**super**
travel agency	**âzhâns-e mosâferat**
vegetable shop	**sabzi forushi**
watchmaker's	**sâ'at sâz**

—Gifts — Hediye-ha

amber	**kahrabâ**
bangle	**alangu**
basket	**sabad**
boots	**chakme**
box	**ja'be**
bracelet	**dastband**
brooch	**senjâgh-e sine**

bowl		**kâse**
candlestick		**sham'-dân**
carpet	*felt*	**named**
	knotted	**farsh**
	woven	**gelim**
	rug	**qâli; qâliche**
chain		**zanjir**
chest		**sandogh**
clock		**sâ'at**
copper		**mes**
crystal		**kristâl; bolur**
curtain		**parde**
cushion	*small*	**kusan**
	large	**motakâ**
earrings		**gushvâre**
emerald		**zomord-e sabz**
gold		**talâ'**
handicraft		**sanâye' dasti**
headscarf		**rusari**
iron		**âhan**
jewelry		**javâher**
kilim		**gelim**
leather		**charm**
metal		**felez**
modern		**modern**
necklace		**gardanband**
pot		**kuzeh**
pottery		**kuzehgari**
ring		**halghe**
rosary		**tasbih**
silver		**noqre**
steel		**fulâd**
stone		**sang**
stool		**chahârpâye**
traditional		**sanati**

tray	**sini**
vase	**goldân**
watch	**sâ'at**
wood	**chub**
wood carvings	**chub-kâri**

—Clothes Lebas

bag	**kif**
belt	**kamarband**
boot	**chakme**
boots	**chakmehâ**
rubber boots	**putinhâ**
bra; brassiere	**sineband**
bracelet	**dastband**
button	**dokme**
buttonhole	**surâkh-e dokme**
cloth	**pârche**
clothes	**lebâs**
coat	**pâlto; mântô**
raincoat	**bârâni**
overcoat	**pâlto**
collar	**yaghe**
cotton	**(parche-ye) nakhi**
dress	**lebâs; pirâhan**
fabric	**pârche**
gloves	**dastkesh**
handbag	**kif**
handkerchief	**dastmâl**
hat	**kolâh**
heel	**pâshne**
jacket	**kôt**
jeans	**jinz**
jumper	**boluz**
leather	**charm**
material	**pârche**

necktie	**kerâvât**
pin	**sanjâgh**
pocket	**jib**
sandal(s)	**sandal(-hâ)**
flipflops	**dampâ'i**
scarf	**shâlgardan**
scissors	**ghaychi**
shawl	**shâl**
shirt	**pirâhan**
shoe(s)	**kafsh(-hâ)**
silk	**abrisham**
silken	**abrishami**
socks	**jurâb**
sole *of shoe*	**zir(-e kafsh)**
suit *men's*	**kôt-o-shalvâr**
women's	**kôt-o-dâman**
stick; walking stick	**asâ**
suit	**kot-o-shalvâr**
sweater	**boluz**
thimble	**angoshtâne**
thread	**nakh**
tights/pantyhose	**jurâb shalvâri**
tie; necktie	**kerâvât**
trousers	**shalvâr**
umbrella/parasol	**chatr**
underwear	**zirpush**
uniform	**uniform**
vest *undershirt*	**zirpush**
waistcoat:	
jacket with sleeves	**zhâkat**
jacket without sleeves	**jelighe**
walking stick	**asâ**
wool	**pashm**
zipper	**zip**

A note on clothing . . .

As Iran is an Islamic Republic, there are laws and customs concerning how people should dress in public. Attire for men is similar to that in most countries. However visitors should note that short trouserss should not be worn outside the house and garden. Short-sleeved shirts are sometimes frowned upon and ties are rarely worn. In most private residences, women can dress in normal western clothes. However in public, covering of the body and hair is obligatory. This consists of a long-sleeved, non-form fitting coat (**rupush** or **mantô**) and a head scarf completely covering the hair, ears and neck (**rusari**; which should be large enough to cover the head and to tie under the chin). Also worn by many women is the **châdor**, a black sheet held under the chin, draping over the head and body. Always be sure to check if your clothing is suitable before venturing out.

—Toiletries

Lavazem-e arayesh

aspirin	**âspirin**
Band-Aid; plaster	**palâster**
brush	**boros**
comb	**shâne**
condom	**kâput**
cotton wool	**panbe**
deodorant	**atr**
hairbrush	**boros**
insect repellant	**hashare kosh**
lipstick	**matik**
mascara	**rimmel**
mouthwash	**mâye'-ye shostoshu-ye dehan**
nail-clippers	**nâkhongir**
nail polish	**lâk**
perfume	**atr**
plaster; Band-Aid	**palâster**
powder	**pudr**
(electric) razor	**rishtarâsh (barghi)**
razor blade	**tigh**

safety pin	**sanjogh ghofli**
sanitary towels	**jan pâk**
shampoo	**shâmpu**
shaving cream	**krem-e rish**
soap	**sâbun**
sponge	**esfânj**
sunblock cream	**krem-e âftâb gereftan**
tampons	**tampôn**
thermometer	**daraje**
tissues	**dastmâl kâghazi**
toilet paper	**dastmâl kâghazi**
toothbrush	**mesvâk**
toothpaste	**khamir dandân**
toothpick	**khalâl dandân**
washing powder *detergent*	**pudr-e lebâs shu'i**

—Stationery

Lavazem-e tahrir

ballpoint	**khodkâr**
book	**ketâb**
dictionary	**farhang**
envelope	**pâkat**
guidebook	**ketâb-e râhnamâ**
ink	**jôhar**
magazine	**majale**
map	**naqshe**
road map	**naqshe-ye râh**
a map of Tehran	**naqshe-ye Tehrân**
newspaper	**ruznâme**
a newspaper in English	**ruznâme be zabân-e Ingilisi**
notebook	**daftarche**
novel	**român**
a novel in English	**român be zabân-e Ingilisi**

paper	**kâghaz**
a piece of paper	**yek tike kâghaz**
pen	**ghalam**
pencil	**madâd**
postcard	**kârt postâl**
scissors	**ghaychi**
writing paper	**kâghaz barâye neveshtan**
Do you have any foreign publications?	**Âyâ shomâ nashriyât-e khâreji dârid?**

—Photography   Aks var dari

How much is it to process (and print) this film?	**Barâye châp kardan-e in film chand mishe?**
When will it be ready?	**Tâ kay âmâde mishavad?**
I'd like film for this camera.	**Man film barâye in durbin mikhâham.**
black and white film	**film-e siyâh o sefid**
camera	**durbin**
color (film)	**film-e rangi**
film	**film**
flash	**felâsh**
lens	**lenz**

—Electrical equipment   Lavazem-barghi

adapter	**âdâptôr**
battery	**bâtri**
cassette	**navâr**
C.D.	**si-di**
C.D. player	**dastgâh-e si-di**
D.V.D.	**di-vi-di**
D.V.D. player	**dastgâh-e di-vi-di**
fan	**havâkesh**

hairdryer	**seshuâr**
iron *for clothing*	**utu**
kettle	**ketri**
plug *two-pin electric*	**dô-shâkhe**
three-pin electric	**seh-shâkhe**
portable T.V.	**televizyon-e dasti**
radio	**radyô**
record	**safe**
tape (cassette)	**navâr**
tape recorder	**zabt**
television	**televizyôn**
transformer	**trânsformer**
videotape	**kaset vidyô**
videotape player	**dastgâh-e vidyô**
voltage regulator	**adâptar**

> **LANGUAGE TIP** — For hi-tech items like cassettes, videos/
> video-players or transformers you are more likely to be
> understood if you use the English terms.

—Sizes   Andaze-ha

small	**kuchek**
big	**bozorg**
heavy	**sangin**
light	**sabok**
more	**bishtar**
less	**kamtar**
many	**ziyâd**
too much/too many	**ziyâd**
enough	**bas; kâfi**
that's enough	**bas ast**
also	**ham**
a little bit	**yek (meghdâr-e) kam**
Do you have a carrier bag?	**Shomâ sâk dârid?**

11. WHAT'S TO SEE
DIDANI-HA

Iran is filled with beautiful cities set in stunning landscapes.. The largest centers after the capital Tehran are Esfahan, Mashhad, Tabriz, Shiraz and Qazvin. Aside from being a teeming metropolis with all the streetlife and cultural institutions you would expect, Tehran is also the logical launch-off point for the rest of the country. Just under two hours' drive from Tehran is Dizin, one of the highest ski resorts in the world, on the slopes of Mount Damavand, a giant dormant volcano 5,600 meters high. The resort gets around seven meters of snow a year. To the north-west is Tabriz, one of the ancient capitals of Iran and famous for its exquisite carpets. Shiraz, the capital of Fars Province, is traditionally known as the "City of Roses and Nightingales". Here you'll find the Eram Garden and the tombs of Saadi and Hafiz – two of the greatest Iranian poets. North of Shiraz lie the immense ruins of fabled Persepolis, begun by by Darius the Great (521-468 B.C.). Esfahan's stunning architecture, tree-lined boulevards and relaxed pace make it the undisputed highlight of Iran's cities — Iranians call it **Nesf-e-Jahân**, meaning "Half The World". Among the world's wonders are its Imam Square (Naqsh-e Jahân) with its Sheikh Lotfollah and Imam Mosques, Alighapu Palace, Chehel Sotun or Forty Pillars Palace, built by Shah Abbas as his audience hall, as well as the most famous bazaar in Iran. There are also the stunning mosques and shrines of the holy cities of Mashhad, capital of Khorasan Province, and the holiest city in Iran (its name means "martyr's burial place"), and Qom where you'll find the exquisite Shrine of Fatima. In contrast, Yazd is laid-back and surrounded by desert. An ancient centre of habitation, it is still an important center of the fire-worhipping Zoroastrians. And you'll find an even greater contrast to the east, near the borders with Pakistan and Afghanistan: Zahedan, the capital of Sistan and Balochestan Province, a city with a wilder, multi-tribal make-up.

Do you have a guide-book?	**Shomâ ketâb-e râhnamâ dârid?**
Do you have a local map?	**Shomâ naghshe-ye mahali dârid?**

Is there a guide who speaks English?	**Râhnamâ'i hast ke Ingilisi balad bâshad?**
What are the main attractions?	**Didâni-hâ chi hast?**
I want to see ...	**Man mikhâham ... râ bebinam.**
We want to see ...	**Mâ mikhâhim ... râ bebinim.**
What is that?	**Ân chi ast?**
How old is it?	**Chand sâl ghadimiyat dârad?**
What animal is that?	**Ân kodâm hayvân ast?**
What fish is that?	**Ân kodâm mâhi-st?**
What insect is that?	**Ân kodâm jânvar ast?**
May I take a photograph?	**Mishe man aks var dâram?**
What time does it open?	**Sâ'at chand bâz mishavad?**
What time does it close?	**Sâ'at chand mibandad?**
What does that sign say?	**Ân neshâne che ma'ni dârad?**
What is this monument/statue?	**In âsâr/mojasame chi ast?**
Who is that statue of?	**In mojasame-ye ki ast?**
Is there an entrance fee?	**Vorudi dârad?**
How much?	**Chand?**
Are there any nightclubs/discos?	**Injâ kolub/diskô hast?**

Note that nightclubs and discos are illegal in Iran.

WHAT'S TO SEE

Where can I hear local folk music?	**Musighi-ye mahali kojâ-st?**
How much does it cost to get in?	**Vorudi chand mishavad?**
What's there to do in the evening?	**Shab-hâ barâye tafrih chi hast?**
Is there a concert?	**Kânsert hast?**
When is the concert?	**Sâ'at chand kânsert shoru' mishavad?**
Where is the wedding?	**Arusi kay hast?**
What time does it begin?	**Sâ'at chand shoru' mishavad?**
Can we swim here?	**Injâ mitavânim shenâ konim?**
Is it safe to get out of the vehicle?	**Khatar nist agar az mâshin khârej shavim?**
Stay in the vehicle!	**Dar mâshin bemân!**
The animals are dangerous.	**In hayvânât khatarnâk hastand.**

—Events

classical music	**musigh-e kelâsik**
concert	**kânsert**
dancing	**raghs**
disco	**diskô**
escalator	**pele barghi**
exhibition	**namâyeshgâh**
folk dancing	**raghs-e mahali**
folk music	**musighi-ye mahali**
jazz	**jâz**
lift/elevator	**âsânsur**
music	**musigh(i)**

party	**mehmâni**
pop music	**musighi-ye pâp**
take-away food/take-out food	**ghazâ ke bâ khod mibarand**

—Venues

academy	**âkâdemi**
apartment	**âpârtemân**
apartment block	**sâkhtemân-e âpârtemân**
archaeological	**bâstâni**
art gallery	**gâleri(-ye honari)**
bakery	**nânvâ'i**
bar	**bâr**
building	**sâkhtemân**
café	**ghahva-khâne; kâfe**
castle	**ghal'e**
cemetery	**ghabrestân**
church	**kelisâ**
cinema	**sinemâ**
city map	**naqshe-ye shahr**
college	**kâlej**
concert	**kânsert**
concert hall	**sâlon-e kânsert**
dispensary	**shafâ khâne**
embassy	**sefârat**
fort	**qal'e; sangar**
hospital	**bimârestân**
house	**khâne**
housing estate/project	**shahrak**
industrial estate	**manteghe-ye san'ati**
library	**ketâbkhâne**
lift/elevator	**âsânsur**
main square	**maydân-e asli**
market	**bâzâr**

monument	**âsâr**
mosque	**masjed**
museum	**muze**
nightclub	**disko**
old city	**shahr-e qadim(i)**
opera house	**tâlâr-e operâ**
park	**pârk**
parliament (building)	**(sâkhtemân-e) majles**
pharmacy	**dârukhâne**
restaurant	**rasturân**
ruins	**âsâr**
saint's tomb	**gur-e moghadas**
school	**madrase**
shop	**maghâze**
shrine	**ziyâratgâh**
stadium	**estadyum**
statue	**mojasame**
store	**maghâze**
street	**khiyâbân**
teahouse	**châykhâne**
temple	**ma'bad**
theatre	**te'âtr**
tomb	**gur**
tower	**borj**
university	**dâneshgâh**
zoo	**bâgh-e vahsh**

—Occasions

birth	**tavalod**
death	**marg**
funeral	**marâsem-e dafn**
wedding	**arusi**
circumcision	**khatne**

12. FINANCE

MAL

CURRENCIES — The official currency in Iran is the **riyâl** (Rl). Every 10 riyâls is known as **1 tômân**, the most commonly used monetary unit.

CHANGING MONEY — Aside from the banks, money can also be changed in any bureau de change, where you will find reliable, up-to-date exchange rates prominently displayed on a board. The cashiers will often know a European language or two, and almost all will show the workings of the exchange on a calculator for you and give you a receipt. Many shops and kiosks will also be happy to change money for you.

I want to change some dollars.	**Mikhâham dolâr tabdil konam.**
I want to change some euros.	**Mikhâham yurô tabdil konam.**
I want to change some pounds.	**Mikhâham pond tabdil konam.**
Where can I change money?	**Kojâ mitivânam arz tabdil konam?**
What is the exchange rate?	**Nerkh-e arz chi ast?**
What is the commission?	**Komisyun cheghadr ast?**
Could you please check that again?	**Inrâ dô martabe chek konid, lotfan.**
Could you write that down for me?	**Mitavânid ân râ barâye man benavisid?**

dollar	**dolâr**
euro	**yuro**
ruble	**rubel**
pound (sterling)	**pond(-e esterling)**

FINANCE

bank notes	**eskenâs-e banki**
bureau de change	**sarâfi**
calculator	**mâshin hesâb**
cashier	**sandughdâr**
coins	**seke**
credit card	**kârt-e e'tebâr**
commission	**komisyun**
exchange	**arz**
foreign exchange/currency	**arz**
loose change	**pul-e khord**
receipt	**resid**
signature	**emzâ**

Courtesy . . .

Iranians pride themselves on being a courteous people and this is reflected in the expressions they use towards guests and superiors. Some related expressions you'll commonly hear and use are:

khôsh âmadid!	welcome!
	To which the response is:
	khôsh bâshid!
khâne âbâd!	may your home be forever!
tashakor!	thank you!
salâmat bâshid!	health to you!
befarmâ'id!	you're welcome!; please!; come to the table!; please eat!; help yourself!
tashrif beyârid!	come again!

13. COMMUNICATIONS
ERTEBAT

—Post
Post

Where is the post office?	**Postkhâne kojâ-st?**
What time does the post office open?	**Postkhâne sâ'at chand bâz mishavad?**
What time does the post office close?	**Postkhâne sâ'at chand mibandad?**
Where is the mail box?	**Sandogh-e post kojâ-st?**
Is there any mail for me?	**Âyâ barâye man nâme âmad?**
How long will it take for this to get there?	**Cheghadr tul mikeshad tâ in beresad?**
How much does it cost to send this to ... ?	**Ferestâdan-e in be ... cheghadr mishavad?**
I would like some stamps.	**Man tambr mikhâstam.**
I would like to send ...	**... mikhâstam beferestam.**
a letter	**yek nâme**
a postcard	**yek kârt postâl**
a parcel	**yek baste**
air mail	**post-e havâ'i**
envelope	**pâkat**
mailbox	**sandogh posti**
to parcel up	**baste-bandi kardan**
registered mail	**post-e sefâreshi**
stamp	**tambr**

—Tele-etiquette

Adab-e telefon

I would like to make a phone call.
Mikhâham yek telefôn konam.

I would like to send a fax.
Mikhâham yek fâks beferestam.

I would like to fax this letter.
Mikhâham in nâme râ fâks konam.

Where is the telephone?
Telefôn kojâ-st?

May I use your phone?
Mitavânam az telefôn-e shomâ estefâde konam?

Can I telephone from here?
Az injâ mitavânam telefôn konam?

Can you help me get this number?
Mitavânid in shomâre râ barâye man begirid?

Can I dial direct?
In shomâre-râ mitavânam mostaghim begiram?

May I speak to Mr. ... ?
Bâ Âqâ-ye ... mitavânam sohbat konam?

May I speak to Mrs./ Miss ... ?
Bâ Khânom-ye ... mitavânam sohbat konam?

Can I leave a message?
Payghâm mitavânam begozâram?

Who is calling, please?
Shomâ, lotfan? or **Jenâb 'âli?**

Who are you calling?
Bâ ki kâr dârid?

Can I take your name?
Esme-tân râ mitavânam beporsam?

Which number are you dialing?
Kodâm shomâre râ gereftid?

He/She is not here at the moment — would you like to leave a message?	**Al'ân nistand, mikhâhid payghâm begozârid?**
This is not ...	**Injâ ... nist.**
You are mistaken.	**Eshtebâh kardid.**
This is the ... office.	**In daftar-e ... ast.**
Hello, I need to speak to ...	**Alô, bâ ... mikhâstam sohbat konam.**
Sorry wrong number.	**Eshtebâ-st.**
I am calling this number ...	**In shomâre-râ mikhâham ...**
I want to ring ...	**Be ... mikhâham zang bezanam.**
Please phone me.	**Lotfan be man zang bezanid.**
What is the code for ... ?	**Kod-e ... chand ast?**
What is the international code for ... ?	**Kod-e baynolmelali barâye ... chand ast?**
What number do I dial for an outside line?	**Barâye khat-e khâreji che shomâra'i râ begiram?**
The number is ...	**Shomâre-sh ... ast.**
The extension is ...	**Dâkheli-sh ... ast.**
It's engaged/busy.	**Eshghâl ast.**
There's no dialing/busy tone.	**Hich sadâ nadârad.**
I've been cut off./The line has been cut off.	**Ghat' shod.**
The telephone is switched off.	**Telefôn khâmush ast.**
Where is the nearest public phone?	**Nazdektarin telefôn-e omumi kojâ-st?**

LANGUAGE TIP — When answering the phone, most people in Iran first say **halô!** or **alô!** — "hello!" You will also hear **bale?** — "yes?"

—Technical words
Loghat-ha-ye fani

digital	**dijitâl**
e-mail	**imayl**
extension (number)	**(shomâre-ye) dâkheli**
fax	**fâks**
fax machine	**dastgâh-e fâks**
handset	**gushi**
international operator	**operâtor-e baynolmelali**
internet	**internet**
internet café	**kafe internet**
line	**khat**
mobile phone; cell phone	**telefôn-e dasti**
modem	**môdem**
operator	**operâtor**
switchboard operator	**telefônchi**
satellite phone	**telefôn-e mâhvâre**
telecommunications	**mokhâberât**
telephone center	**markaz-e telefôn/ mokhâberât**
to transfer/put through	**vasl kardan**

—Faxing & e-mailing
Faks o emayl

Where can I send a fax from?	**Az kojâ mitavânam fâks beferestam?**
Can I fax from here?	**Az injâ mitavânam fâks beferestam?**

How much is it to fax?	**Fâks kardan cheghadr mishavad?**
Where can I find a place to e-mail from?	**Az kojâ mitavânam emayl beferestam?**
Is there an internet café near here?	**Nazdik-e injâ kâfe internet hast?**
Can I e-mail from here?	**Az injâ mitavânam emayl beferestam?**
How much is it to use a computer?	**Chand mishavad baraye estefâde kardan-e kâmpyuter?**
How do you turn on this computer?	**In kâmpyuter chetôr rôshan mishavad?**
The computer has crashed.	**Kâmpyuter az kâr oftâd.**
I need help with this computer.	**Bâ in kâmpyuter komak ehtiyâj dâram.**
I don't know how to use this program.	**Nemidânam chetôr bâ in barnâme kâr konam.**
I know how to use this program.	**Man midânam chetôr bâ in barnâme kâr konam.**
I want to print.	**Mikhâham châp konam.**

14. THE OFFICE
EDARE

chair	**sandali**
computer	**kâmpyuter**
desk	**miz**
drawer	**keshô**
fax	**fâks**
file *paper/computer*	**parvande**
meeting: *of two people*	**molâqât**
of a larger group	**jalase**
paper	**kâghaz**
pen biro	**khodkâr**
fountain pen	**ghalam**
pencil	**madâd**
photocopier	**dastgâh-e fotokopi**
photocopy	**fotokopi**
printer	**printer**
(computer) program	**barnâme (-ye kâmpyuter)**
report	**gozâresh**
ruler	**khatkesh**
scanner	**eskaner**
telephone	**telefôn**
typewriter	**mâshin-tahrir**

15. THE CONFERENCE
KANFERANS

agenda	**âzhendâ**
article	**maqâle**
a break *for refreshments*	**tafrih**
chairman/chairwoman	**ra'is**
conference	**kânfarâns**
conference room	**otâgh-e kânfarâns**
copy	**noskhe**
discussion	**bahs**
guest speaker	**mehmân-e sokhanrân**
a (written) paper	**maghâle**
podium	**sakn**
projector	**prozhektar**
session	**jalase**
a session chaired by ...	**jalase'i taht-e riyâsat-e ...**
speaker	**sokhanrân**
subject	**mavzu'**
translation	**tarjome**
translator	**motarjem**

16. EDUCATION
AMUZESH O PARVARESH

to add	**jam' kardan**
addition	**jam'**
bench	**nimkat**
biro	**khodkâr**
blackboard	**takhte siyâh**
book	**ketâb**
calculation	**mohâsebe**
chalk	**gach**
class	**kelâs**
to copy	**kâpi kardan**
to count	**shomârdan**
crayon	**madâd sham'i**
difficult	**sakht**
to divide	**taqsim kardan**
division	**taqsim**
easy	**âsân**
eraser	**pâk-kon**
exam	**emtehân**
exercise book	**daftarche**
to explain	**tôzih dâdan**
felt-tip pen	**mâzhik**
geography	**joghrâfi**
glue	**chasp**
grammar	**dastur zabân**
history	**târikh**
holidays	**ta'tilât**
homework	**mashgh**
illiterate	**bisavâd**
language	**zabân**
laziness	**tambali**

to learn	**yâd gereftan**
to learn by heart	**az bar yâd gereftan**
lesson	**dars**
library	**ketâbkhâne**
literature	**adabiyât**
madrasa	**madrase**
maths	**riyâzi**
memory	**hefz**
multiplication	**zarb**
to multiply	**zarb kardan**
notebook	**daftarche**
page	**safhe**
paper	**kâghaz**
to pass *an exam*	**ghabul shodan**
pen	**ghalam; khodkâr**
pencil	**madâd**
progress	**pishraft**
to punish	**tanbih kardan**
pupil	**shâgerd**
to read	**khândan**
to repeat	**tekrâr kardan**
rubber *eraser*	**pâk-kon**
ruler *instrument*	**khatkesh**
satchel	**kif(-e madrase)**
school	**madrase**
sheet *of paper*	**varaqe**
slate	**lôh**
student *university*	**dâneshju**
to subtract	**menhâ kardan**
subtraction	**menhâ**
sum	**hesâb**
table	**miz**
teacher	**mo'alem**
test *academic*	**emtchân; âzemun**
to test *academic*	**emtehân/âzemun kardan**

17. AGRICULTURE
KESHAVARZI

agriculture	**keshâvarzi**
barley	**jô**
barn	**anbâr**
cattle	**gale-ye gav**
to clear *land*	**pâk kardan**
combine harvester	**kambâyn**
corn	**ghale**
cotton	**panbe**
crops	**mahsul**
to cultivate	**kesht kardan**
earth *land*	**zamin**
soil	**khâk**
fallowland	**zamin-e bâyer**
farm	**mazra'e**
farmer	**keshâvarz**
farming	**keshâvarzi**
to feed an animal	**khorâk dâdan**
(animal) feed	**khorâk**
fertilizer	**kud**
field	**mazra'e**
fruit	**mive**
garden	**bâgh**
grass	**chaman**
to grind	**âsyâb kardan**
to grow *crops*	**sabz shodan**
harvest	**kharman**
hay	**alaf-e khoshk**
irrigation	**âbyâri**
leaf	**barg**
livestock	**chahâr pâyân-e asli**

maize	**zorat**
manure	**kud**
marsh	**mordâb**
meadow	**marghzâr**
to milk *an animal*	**dushidan**
mill	**âsyâb**
orchard	**bâgh-e mive**
to plant	**kâshtan**
plow	**gâv-e âhan**
to plow	**shokhm zadan**
potato	**sib-zamini**
poultry	**morghân-e khânegi**
to reap	**darô kardan**
rice	**berenj**
root	**rishe**
rye	**gandom-e siyâh**
season	**fasl**
seeds	**tokhm**
to shoe *a horse*	**na'l kardan**
silkworm(s)	**kerm-e abrisham**
to sow	**afshândan**
straw	**kâh**
tractor	**terâktôr**
tree	**derakht**
trunk *of tree*	**tane**
well (of water)	**châh**
wheat	**gandom**

18. ANIMALS
HAYVANAT

—Mammals

animal	**hayvân**
animals	**hayvânât**
antelope	**gavazn**
bat	**khofâsh**
bear	**khers**
boar	**gorâz**
buffalo	**bufâlô**
bull	**gâv-e nar**
calf	**gusâle**
camel	**shotor**
cat	**gorbe**
cow	**gâv**
deer	**âhu; gavazn**
dog	**sag**
Beware of the dog!	**Movâzeb-e sag bâshid!**
donkey	**khar**
elephant	**fil**
ewe	**mish**
ferret	**râsu**
flock *of sheep*	**gale**
fox	**rubâh**
gazelle	**ghazâl**
goat	**boz**
herd	**gale**
horse	**asb**
jackal	**shaghal**
lamb	**bare**
leopard	**palang**

lion	**shir**
mare	**mâdiyân**
mole	**kurmush**
mongoose	**peshak-e vahshi**
monkey	**maymun**
mouse	**mush**
mule	**ghâter**
ox	**gâv-e nar**
pig	**khuk**
pony	**kore-ye asb**
rabbit	**khargush**
ram	**ghuch**
rat	**mush-e sahrâ'i**
sheep	**gusfand**
sheepdog	**sag-e gale**
squirrel	**sanjâb**
stag	**gavazn-e nar**
stallion	**asb-e nar**
wolf	**gorg**

—Birds

bird	**parande**
birds	**parande-gân**
chicken/hen	**morgh**
cock/rooster	**khorus**
crow	**kalâgh**
dove	**kabutar**
duck	**morghâbi**
eagle	**oghâb**
falcon	**shâhin**
goose	**ghâz**
hawk	**bâz**
hen	**morgh**
nightingale	**bolbol**

ANIMALS

owl	**buf**
parrot	**tuti**
partridge	**kabk**
peacock	**tâvus**
pheasant	**gharghâvol**
pigeon	**kabutar**
quail	**baldarchin**
rooster	**khorus**
sparrow	**gonjeshk**
turkey	**morgh-e hendi**
vulture	**lâshkhur**

—Insects & amphibians

ant(s)	**murche**
bee	**zanbur**
butterfly	**parvâne**
caterpillar	**kerm-e sad-pâ**
cobra	**mâr-e kôbrâ**
cockroach	**susk**
crab	**kharchang**
cricket	**jirjirak**
dragonfly	**sanjâghok**
firefly	**kerm-e shab tâb**
fish	**mâhi**
flea(s)	**kayk(-hâ)**
fly	**magas**
frog	**ghurbâghe**
gecko	**mârmulak**
grasshopper	**malakh**
hedgehog	**khârposht**
hornet	**zanbur-e sorkh**
insect	**hashare**
insects	**hasharât**
lizard	**susmâr**

louse	**shepesh**
lice	**shepesh-hâ**
mosquito(es)	**pashe(-hâ)**
scorpion	**aqrab**
snail	**halazun**
snake	**mâr**
spider	**ankabut**
sturgeon	**mâhi-ye khâvyâr**
termite	**muryâne**
tick	**kane**
tortoise; turtle	**sang posht**
viper	**tirmâr**
wasp	**zanbur**
worm(s)	**kerm(-hâ)**

19. COUNTRYSIDE
YILAGHAT

avalanche	**bahman**
canal	**kânâl**
cave	**ghâr**
dam	**sad**
desert	**sahrâ**
earth	**zamin**
earthquake	**zelzele**
fire	**âtesh**
flood	**sayl**
foothills	**dâmane-ye kuh**
footpath	**râh-e 'obur**
forest	**jangal**
hill	**tape**
lake	**daryâche**
landslide	**âbroft**
marsh	**mordâb**
mountain	**kuh**
mountain pass	**gozargâh-e kuhi**
mountain range	**selsele-ye kuhi**
peak	**nôk**
plain/plains	**dasht**
plant	**giyâh**
pond	**hôz**
ravine	**dare-tand; darband**
river	**rudkhâne**
river bank	**lab-e rudkhâne**
rock	**sang**
sand	**mâse**
slope	**dâmane**
soil	**khâk**

spring of water	**sarchesme**
stone	**sang**
stream	**rud; juy-e âb**
summit	**nôk; ghale**
swamp	**mordâb**
torrent	**saylâb**
tree	**derakht**
valley	**dare**
waterfall	**âb shâr**
a wood	**jangal**

20. WEATHER

HAVA

What's the weather like?	**Havâ chetor ast?**

The weather is ... today.	**Emruz havâ ... ast.**
cold	**sard**
cool/fresh	**khonak/tâze**
cloudy	**abri**
foggy	**meh-âlud**
freezing	**yakh bandân**
hot	**garm**
misty	**meh**
very hot	**khayli garm**
very cold	**khayli sard**

It's going to rain.	**Bârân khâhad beyâd.**
It is raining.	**Bârân miyâd.**
It's going to snow.	**Barf khâhad beyâd.**
It's becoming very cold.	**Dârad khayli sard mishavad.**
It is snowing.	**Barf miyâd**
It is sunny.	**Âftâbi miyâd.**
It is windy.	**Bâd miyâd.**

—Weather words

Loghat-ha-ye ab o hava

air	**havâ**
climate	**âb o havâ**
cloud	**abr**

blizzard	**bâd-e shadid bâ barf**
dew	**shabnam**
drought	**khoshk sâli**
famine	**ghahti**
fog	**meh**
to freeze	**yakh bastan**
frost	**yakh bandân**
glacier	**yakh-rud**
hail	**tagarg**
hailstorm	**tufân-e tagarg**
heatwave	**garmâ-ye fôghul'âde**
ice	**yakh**
lightning	**bargh**
lightning bolt	**mile-ye barghgir**
mist	**meh**
moon	**mâh**
new moon	**helâl-e mâh**
full moon	**ghors-e mâh**
planet	**sayâre**
rain	**bârân**
rainbow	**rangin kamân**
shower *of rain*	**ragbâr**
sky	**âsemân**
snow	**barf**
snowflakes	**dane-ye barf**
snowdrift	**barf-e anbâshta**
star	**setâre**
stars	**setâre-gân**
storm	**tufân**
thunderstorm	**ra'd o bargh**
sun	**âftâb**
to thaw	**âb shodan**
thunder	**ra'd**

WEATHER

weather	**havâ**
wind	**bâd**

—Seasons	Fasl-ha
spring	**bahâr**
summer	**tâbestân**
autumn; fall	**pâ'iz**
winter	**zemestân**

Horoscope . . .
Here are the names of the star signs:

Hamal	Aries
Sôr	Taurus
Jôzâ	Gemini
Saratân	Cancer
Asad	Leo
Sunbule	Virgo
Mizân	Libra
Aghrab	Scorpio
Ghôs	Sagittarius
Jadi	Capricorn
Dalv	Aquarius
Hut	Pisces

21. CAMPING
CHADOR ZADAN

Where can we camp?	**Kojâ mitunim châdor bezanim?**
Can we camp here?	**Injâ mitunim châdor bezanim?**
Is it safe to camp here?	**Barâye châdor zadan injâ amniyat dâre?**
Is there danger of wild animals?	**Âyâ dar injâ khatar-e hayvânat-e vahshi vojud dârad?**
Is there drinking water?	**Âb-e khordan hast?**
May we light a fire?	**Mishe âtesh rôshan konim?**

—Kit

ax	**tabar**
backpack	**kul-e poshti**
bucket	**satl**
campsite	**jâ-ye châdor zadan**
can opener	**darbâz kon**
compass	**qotbnamâ**
firewood	**hizom**
flashlight	**cherâgh ghove**
gas canister	**kâpsul-e gâz**
hammer	**chakosh**
ice ax; ice pick	**yakhshekan**
ice-box	**yakhchâl**
lamp	**cherâgh**
mattress	**toshak**
penknife	**châqu-ye kuchek-e jibi**
rope	**tanâb**

CAMPING

sleeping bag	**kise khâb**
stove: *cooking*	**fer-e khorâk pazi**
heating	**bukhâri**
tent	**châdor**
tent pegs	**gire-ye châdor**
water bottle	**botri-ye âb**

Weights & measures . . .

Iran uses the metric system. Here is a list of international units — for reference, translations are included for the most common imperial units:

kilometer	**kilometr**
meter	**metr**
mile	**mâyl**
foot	**fut**
yard	**yârd**
acre	**ayker**
gallon	**gâlôn**
liter	**litr**
kilogram	**kilogrâm**
ton; tonne	**ton**
pound	**pond**
gram	**grâm**
ounce	**âns**

Two traditional words used for units of distance in Iran are the the **farsang** or **farsakh-song**, usually equal to 6.24 kilometers (about 3.88 miles), and the metric **farsang**, equal to 10 kilometers (approximately 6.2 miles).

22. EMERGENCY
VAZE' EZTERARI

COMPLAINING — If you really feel you have been cheated or misled, raise the matter first with your host or the proprietor of the establishment in question preferably with a smile. Iranians are proud but courteous, with a deeply felt tradition of hospitality, and consider it their duty to help any guest. Angry glares and shouting will get you nowhere.

CRIME — Without undue paranoia, take usual precautions: watch your wallet or purse, securely lock your equipment and baggage before handing it over to railway or airline porters, and don't leave valuables on display in your hotel room. On buses, look out for pickpockets – keep valuables in front pockets and your bag close to your side. If you are robbed, contact the police. Of course in the more remote areas, sensible precautions should be taken, and always ensure that you go with a guide. In general, follow the same rules as you would in your own country and you will run little risk of encountering crime.

LOST ITEMS — If you lose something, save time and energy by appealing only to senior members of staff or officials. If you have lost items in the street or left anything in public transport, the police may be able to help.

DISABLED FACILITIES — The terrain and conditions throughout most of Iran do not make it easy for any visitor in a wheelchair or with mobility difficulties to get around even at the best of times. Access to most buildings in the towns is difficult, particularly since the majority of lifts function irregularly. Facilities are rarely available in hotels, airports or other public areas.

wheelchair	**sandali-ye charkhdâr**
disabled person	**ma'alul**
disabled people	**ma'alulin**
Do you have seats for the disabled?	**Barâye ma'alulin jâ dârid?**
Do you have access for the disabled?	**Râh dârid barâye ma'alulin?**
Do you have facilities for the disabled?	**Emkânât dârid barâye ma'alulin?**

Help!	**Komak!**
Could you help me, please?	**Lotfan marâ komak mikonid?**
Do you have a telephone?	**Shomâ telefôn dârid?**
Can I use your telephone?	**Mitunam az telefôn-e shomâ estefade konam?**
Where is the nearest telephone?	**Nazdiktarin telefôn kojâ-st?**
Does the phone work?	**Telefôn kâr mikonad?**
Get help quickly!	**Sari' komak bekhâhid!**
Call the police.	**Be polis khabar bedehid.**
I'll call the police!	**Man bâ polis tamâs migiram!**
Is there a doctor near here?	**Doktôr hast nazdik-e injâ?**
Call a doctor.	**Doktôr râ sedâ konid.**
Call an ambulance.	**Âmbulâns râ sedâ konid.**
I'll get medical help!	**Komak-e tebi migiram!**
Where is the doctor?	**Doktôr kojâ-st?**
Is there a doctor?	**Doktôr hast?**
Where is the hospital?	**Bimârestân kojâ-st?**
Where is the pharmacy?	**Dârukhâne kojâ-st?**
Where is the dentist?	**Dandânsâz kojâ-st?**
Where is the police station?	**Kalântari kojâ-st?**
Take me to a doctor.	**Marâ pish-e doktôr bebarid.**

There's been an accident!	**Tasâdof shode!**
Is anyone hurt?	**Kasi turi shode?**
This person is hurt.	**In shakhs zakhm shode.**
There are people injured.	**Chand nafar zakhm shodand.**
Don't move!	**Tekân nakôrid!**
Go away!	**Berid!**
Stand back!	**Aghab vâ'isid!**
I am lost.	**Man gom shodam.**
I am ill.	**Man mariz am.**
I've been robbed.	**Marâ dozd zade.**
Thief!	**Dozd!**
My ... has been stolen.	**...-e man dozdi shode.**
I have lost ...	**... gom shode.**
my bags	**bagâzh-am**
my camera equipment	**lavâzem-e film-vardâri-ye-man**
my handbag	**kif-am**
my laptop computer	**kâmpyuter-am**
my money	**pul-am**
my passport	**pâspôrt-am**
my traveler's checks	**terâvelchek-hâ-m**
my wallet	**kif-e pul-am**
My possessions are insured.	**Vasâ'el-e-man bime hast.**
I have a problem.	**Man moshkel dâram.**
I didn't do it.	**Kâr-e man nabud.**
I'm sorry.	**Mota'asefam.**
I apologize.	**Ma'azerat mikham.**
I didn't realize anything was wrong.	**Man motavajeh nabudam ke eshkâli bud.**

I want to contact my embassy/consulate.	**Mikhâm bâ sefârat-am tamâs begiram.**
I speak English.	**Man Ingilisi sohbat mikonam.**
I need an interpreter.	**Ehteyâj be motarjem dâram.**
Where are the toilets/bathrooms?	**Dast shu'i kojâ-st?**

23. HEALTHCARE
SALAMAT

What's the trouble?	**Moshkel-e shomâ chi-st?**
I am sick.	**Man mariz am.**
My companion is sick.	**Hamrâh-e man mariz e.**
May I see a female doctor?	**Momken ast doktôr-e zan bebinam?**
I have medical insurance.	**Bime-ye tebi dâram.**
Please take off your shirt.	**Lotfan pirâhan-etân râ darârid.**
Please take off your clothes.	**Lotfan lebâs-etân râ darârid.**
What's the problem?	**Moshkel-etân chi ast?**
How long have you had this problem?	**In moshkel râ chand vaght dârid?**
How long have you been feeling sick?	**Chand vaght ehsâs-e marizi dârid?**
Have you been ill before?	**Ghablan mariz shodid?**
How many times?	**Chand dafe?**
Where does it hurt?	**Kojâ dard dârid?**
It hurts here.	**Injâ dard mikone.**
Where?	**Kojâ?**
Here.	**Injâ.**
That hurts.	**Dard mikone.**
For how many days?	**Chand ruz mishe?**

I have been vomiting.	**Estefrâgh mikardam.**
I feel dizzy.	**Sar-am gich mire.**
I can't eat.	**Nemitunam ghazâ bokhôram.**
I can't sleep.	**Nemitunam bekhâbam.**
I fell.	**Oftâdam.**
I had an accident.	**Man tasâdof kardam.**
I feel worse.	**Hâlem badtar e.**
I feel better.	**Hâlem behtar e.**
Do you have diabetes?	**Bimâri-ye shekar dârid?**
Do you have epilepsy?	**Bimâri-ye sar' dârid?**
Do you have asthma?	**Tangi-ye nafas dârid?**
I have diabetes.	**Man bimâri-ye shekar dâram.**
I have epilepsy.	**Man bimâri-ye sar' dâram.**
I have asthma.	**Man nafas-tangi dâram.**
I'm pregnant.	**Man hâmele hastam.**
How many children do you have?	**Chand tâ bache dârid?**
I have one child.	**Yek bache dâram.**
I have two/three/four children.	**Dô/seh/chahâr bache dâram.**
I have a cold.	**Sarmâ khordam.**

You *(formal)* have a cold.	**Sarmâ khordid.**
You *(informal)* have a cold.	**Sarmâ khordi.**
I have a cough.	**Sorfe mikonam.**
You *(formal)* have a cough.	**Sorfe mikonid.**
You *(informal)* have a cough.	**Sorfe mikoni.**
I have a headache.	**Saram dard mikone.** *or* **Sardard dâram.**
You *(formal)* have a headache.	**Sardard dârid.**
You *(informal)* have a headache.	**Sardard dâri.**
I have ...	**Man ... dâram.**
You *(formal)* have ...	**Shomâ ... dârid.**
You *(informal)* have ...	**Tô ... dâri.**
a pain	**dard**
a sore throat/tonsils	**gelu dard/tânsal**
a temperature	**tab**
an allergy	**hasâsiyat**
an infection	**ofunat**
a rash	**jush**
backache	**kamar dard**
constipation	**yobs**
diarrhea	**es-hâl**
fever	**tab**
hepatitis	**hepâtit**
indigestion	**rudel**
influenza	**ânfluenzâ**
a heart condition	**maraz-e ghalbi**
stomachache	**deldard**
a fracture	**shekastagi**
toothache	**dandân dard**

It itches here.	**Injâ mikhârad.**
I have pins and needles in my ...	**...-am khâb rafte.**
I take this medication.	**In davâ râ mikhoram.**
I need medication for ...	**In davâ râ barâye ... ihtiyâj dâram.**
What type of medication is this?	**In che nô'i dârust?**
What pill is this?	**In mosaken chist?**
How many times a day must I take it?	**Ruzi chand bâr bâyad in-ô bokhoram?**
When should I stop my medicine?	**Kay davâm râ qat' konam?**
I'm on antibiotics.	**Ântibiyotik mikhoram.**
I'm allergic to antibiotics.	**Be ântibiyotik hasâsiyat dâram.**
I'm allergic to penicillin.	**Be penisilin hasâsiyat dâram.**
I have been vaccinated.	**Vâksan shodam.**
I have my own syringe.	**Sôranj-e khodam râ dâram.**
Is it possible for me to travel?	**Mitunam mosâferat konam?**

—Eyesight

Binayi

I have broken my glasses.	**Aynak-am shekaste.**
Can you repair them?	**Mitunid dorost konid?**
I need new lenses.	**Man niyâz be lenz hâye nav dâram.**
When will they be ready?	**Kay hâzer mishe?**

How much do I owe you?	**Cheghadr mishe?**
sunglasses	**aynak âftâbi**
glasses; eyeglasses	**aynak**
contact lenses	**lenz**
contact lens solution	**mâye'-ye shostan-e lenz**

—Health words
Loghat-ha-ye salamat

AIDS	**aydz**
airsick	**marizi-ye parvâz**
I am airsick.	**Man marizi-ye parvâz dâram.**
alcoholism	**e'tiyâdi be alkol**
altitude sickness	**bimâri-ye ertefâ**
to amputate	**qat'-e andâm kardan**
anemia	**kam khuni**
anesthetic	**davâ-ye bihushi**
anesthetist	**pezeshk-e motakhases-e bihushi**
antibiotic	**ântibiyotik**
antiseptic	**zed-e ofuni**
appetite	**eshtehâ**
artery	**rag**
artifical arm	**dast-e masnu'i**
artifical eye	**cheshm-e masnu'i**
artifical leg	**pâ-ye masnu'i**
aspirin	**âspirin**
bandage	**bând**
bandaid *plaster*	**chasp**
better	**behtar**
bite	**nish**
insect bite	**nish-e hashare**

mosquito bite	**nish-e pashe**
snakebite	**nish-e mâr**
This insect bit me.	**In hashare marâ nish karde.**
This snake bit me.	**In mâr marâ nish karde.**
bladder	**masâne**
blood	**khun**
blood group	**grup-e khun**
blood pressure:	**feshâr-e khun**
high blood pressure	**feshâr-e bâlâ**
low blood pressure	**feshâr-e pâ'in**
blood transfusion	**enteqâl-e khun**
bone	**ostokhun**
brain	**maghz**
bug *insect*	**jânevar**
burn *noun*	**suzesh**
cancer	**saretân**
choke	**khafe shodan**
He/She is choking!	**Khafe mishavad!**
cholera	**kolerâ**
clinic	**klinik**
cold *medical*	**sarmâ khordegi**
constipation	**yobs**
Are you constipated?	**Yobs hastid?**
cotton wool	**panbe**
cough	**sorfe**
cream *ointment*	**krem**
crutch	**chub dasti**
dehydration	**kam shodan-e âb-e badan**
dentist	**dandân-sâz**
diarrhea	**es-hâl**
diet	**rezhim**
dressing *medical*	**bândâzh**

drug	*medical*	**davâ; dâru**
	narcotic	**mavâd-e mokhadar**
dysentery		**es-hâl khuni**
ear		**gush**
ears		**gush-hâ**
ear drum		**tabl-e gush**
edema		**varam**
epidemic		**nâkhoshi-ye hamehgir**
eye		**cheshm**
eyes		**cheshm-hâ**
femur		**ostokhun-e rân**
fever		**tab**
flea		**kek**
flu		**ânfluyenzâ**
food poisoning		**masmumiyat-e ghazâ**
I ate this.		**Man in râ khordam.**
frostbite		**yakh zadagi**
gall bladder		**kise-ye sofrâ**
gently!		**yavâsh!**
germs		**mikrôb-hâ**
gut		**rude**
hand		**dast**
right hand		**dast-e râst**
left hand		**dast-e chap**
hard! *vigorously*		**seft!**
health		**salâmat**
heart attack		**sakte-ye qalbi**
heatstroke		**âftâb zadegi**
heel		**pâshne**
hip		**mafsal-e rân**
hips		**mafsal-hâ-ye rân**
HIV		**ech-ây-vi**
hygiene		**hefz-o-seha**

infant	**kudak; bache**
infection	**ofuniyat**
It is infected.	**Ofuniyat karde.**
insect	**jânevar**
intestine(s)	**rude(-hâ)**
joint	**mafsal**
kidney	**koliye**
kidneys	**koliye-hâ**
lice	**shepesh**
limbs	**andâm-hâ**
malaria	**mâlâryâ**
maternity hospital	**bimârestân-e hâmele**
milk: *mother's*	**shir-e mâdar**
cow's	**shir-e gâv**
goat's	**shir-e boz**
powdered	**shir-e pudr**
mouth	**dehan**
muscle	**azule**
navel	**nâf**
needle	**suzan**
nerve	**asab**
newborn child	**bache nô-zâd**
nose	**bini**
nurse	**parastâr**
ointment *cream*	**rôghan; krem**
operating theatre/room	**otâgh-e amal**
(surgical) operation	**amal**
organ *of body*	**ozv**
oxygen	**âksizhen**
pain	**dard**
painkiller	**mosaken**
palm *of hand*	**kaf-e dast**
pancreas	**lôz-ul-me'de**
physiotherapy	**fiziyoterâpi**
placenta	**joft**

plaster: *bandaid*	**chasp**
cast	**palâster**
pupil *of eye*	**mardomak-e chesm**
rabies	**hâri**
rib(s)	**dande(-hâ)**
ribcage	**qafase-ye sine**
saliva	**âb-e dehan**
shoulder-blade	**ostokhun-e shâne**
shrapnel	**shrapnel**
side *of body*	**taraf**
skin	**pust**
skull	**jomjome; kâse-ye sar**
sleeping pill	**ghors-e khâb**
snowblindness	**barf kuri**
sole *of foot*	**kaf-e pâ**
spinal column; spine	**nakhâ'**
spots	**jush-hâ**
stethoscope	**gushi-ye tebi**
stroke	**sakte-ye maghzi**
sunstroke	**âftâb zadegi**
surgeon	**jarâh**
(act of) surgery	**amaliyât; amal**
syringe	**sôranj**
syrup *medical*	**sharbat**
thermometer	**damâsanj**
thigh	**rân**
thorax	**(ghafase-ye) sine**
throat	**gelu**
tibia	**ghasaba'i kubrâ**
tooth	**dandân**
teeth	**dandân-hâ**
torture	**shekanje**
trachea	**ghasaba ar-ri'a**
tranquilizer	**mosâken**
tuberculosis	**sel**

HEALTHCARE

umbilical cord	**band-e nâf**
umbilicus	**nâf**
urine	**miz**
vein	**rag**
vertebra	**fighra**
vitamins	**vitâmin-hâ**
to vomit	**estefrâgh kardan**
waist	**kamar**
windpipe	**ghasaba ar-ri'a**

24. RELIEF AID
KOMAK-E EMDADI

Can you help me?	**Mitavânid man-ô komak konid?**
Do you speak English?	**Ingilisi sohbat mikonid?**
Who is in charge?	**Mas'ul-e injâ ki ye?**
Fetch the main person in charge.	**Mas'ul-e injâ râ biyârid.**
What's the name of this town?	**Esm-e in shahr chi ye?**
How many people live here/there?	**Chand kas injâ/ânjâ manzel dârand?**
earthquake	**zelzele**
after-shock	**za'f-e ba'di**
Is there anyone injured?	**Chand nafar zakhm shodand?**
Is there anyone trapped?	**Kesi gir karde?**
How many survivors are there?	**Chand bâzmânde-gân hastand?**
Where?	**Kojâ?**
How many are missing?	**Chand kas gom shode?**
Who?	**Ki?**
What are their names?	**Esm-hâ-ye-ishân chi-yand?**
Keep quiet!	**Sâket!**
Can you hear a sound?	**Sedâ miyâd?**
I can hear a sound.	**Sedâ mishanavam.**

Under that building.	**Zir-e ân sakhtemân.**
Help me clear the rubble!	**Shomâ be-khârabi-ye bardâshtan komak konid!**
Danger!	**Khatar!**
It's going to collapse!	**Miyoftâd!**
sniffer dog	**sag-e buyâyi**
What's the name of that river?	**Esm-e ân rudkhâne chi ye?**
How deep is it?	**Omgh-esh cheghadr e?**
Is the bridge still standing?	**Pol sar-e jâ-st?**
Is the bridge down?	**Pol kharâb shod?**
Where can we ford the river?	**Kojâ mitunim az rudkhâne gozar konim?**
What is the name of that mountain?	**Esm-e ân kuh chi ye?**
How high is it?	**Chand metr ertefâ' dârad?**
Where is the border?	**Marz kojâ-st?**
Is it safe?	**Khatar nadârad?**
Show me.	**Neshân-am bedid.**

—Security Amniyat

checkpoint	**istgâh-e bâzrasi-ye marz**
roadblock	**râhbandân**
Stop!	**Vâ'isin!**
Do not move!	**Harekat nakonid!**
Go!	**Berid!**
Who are you?	**Shomâ ki hastid?**
Don't shoot!	**Shelik nakonid!**
Help!	**Komak!**
Help me!	**Man-ô komak konid!**

no entry	**vorud mamnu'**
emergency exit	**khoruj-e esterâri**
straight on	**mostaghim**
turn left	**dast-e chap bepich**
turn right	**dast-e râst bepich**
this way	**in var**
that way	**ân var**
Keep quiet!	**Sâket!**
You are right.	**Râst migid.**
You are wrong.	**Eshtebâh mikonid.**
I am ready.	**Hâzer am.**
I am in a hurry.	**Ajale dâram.**
Well, thank you!	**Khob, tashakor!**
What's that?	**Ân chi ye?**
Come in!	**Befârma'id!**
That's all!	**Bas e!** *or* **Hamin!**

—Food distribution
Tozi'-ye ghaza

feeding station	**markaz-e âzughe**
Please form a queue there/here.	**Lotfan injâ/ânjâ saf bebandid.**
How many people are in your family?	**Khânevâde-ye shomâ chand nafar and?**
How many children?	**Chand tâ bache?**
You must come back this ...	**... bâyad bargadid.**
afternoon	**ba'd az zohr**
tonight	**emshab**
tomorrow	**fardâ**
the day after	**pasfardâ**
next week	**hafte-ye ba'd**
There is water for you.	**Barâye shomâ âb hast.**
There is grain for you.	**Barâye shomâ gandom hast.**

There is food for you.	**Barâye shomâ ghazâ ast.**
There is fuel for you.	**Barâye shomâ sukht ast.**

—Road repair
Ta'amir-e rah kardan

Is the road passable?	**In râh ghâbel-e obur hast?**
Is the road blocked?	**In râh masdud ast?**
We are repairing the road.	**Jâde dar dast-e ta'mir ast.**
We are repairing the bridge.	**Pol dar dast-e ta'mir ast.**
We need ...	**... ehtiyâj dârim.**
wood	**chub**
a rock	**sang**
rocks	**sang-hâ**
gravel/sand	**shen**
fuel	**sukht**
Lift!	**Boland konid!**
Drop it!	**Vel-esh konid!**
Now!	**Hâlâ!**
All together!	**Hame bâ ham!** or **Yâ 'ali!**

—Mines
Min-ha

mine *noun*	**min**
mines	**min-hâ**
minefield	**mantaghe-ye min**
	gozâri kardan
to lay mines	**min gozâri kardan**
to hit a mine	**ru-ye min raftan**
to clear a mine	**min râ khonsâ kardan**

mine detector	**min yâb**
mine disposal	**minbardâri**
Are there any mines near here?	**In havâli min hast?**
What type are they?	**Che nô' min hastand?**
anti-vehicle	**zed-e mâshin**
anti-personnel	**zed-e persônel**
plastic	**pelâstik**
floating	**shenâvar**
magnetic	**âhan robâ'i**
What size are they?	**Che andâze'i hastand?**
What color are they?	**Che rangi hastand?**
Are they marked?	**Neshane'i dârand?**
How?	**Che neshâne'i?**
How many mines are there?	**Chand tâ min dâre?**
When were they laid?	**Kay gozâshte budand?**
Can you take me to the minefields?	**Mitunid marâ tâ naz-dik-e mantaghe-hâ-ye min gozâri shode bebarid?**
Are there any (exploded) booby traps near there?	**Ân havâli min-e tale (enfejâri shode) hast?**
Are they made from grenades, high explosives or something else?	**Bâ nârenjak, sukhtâr yâ chiz-e digar dorost shode?**
Are they in a building?	**Dâkhel-e sâkhtemân hastand?**
on tracks?	**sar-e râh?**
on roads?	**sar-e jâde?**
on bridges?	**sar-e pol?**
or elsewhere?	**yâ jâ-ye dige?**
Can you show me?	**Mitunid be man neshân bedid?**

| Don't touch that! | **Dast nazan!** |
| Don't go near that! | **Nazdik-e ân narô!** |

—Other useful words

Loghat-ha-ye mofid-e digar

airdrop	**ghoyud**
airforce	**niru-ye havâ'i**
ambulance	**âmbulâns**
armored car	**nafarbar**
army	**artesh**
artillery	**tupkhâne**
barbed wire	**sim-e khârdâr**
bomb	**bômb**
cluster bomb	**bômb-e khoshe'i**
bomber plane	**tayâre-ye jangi**
bullet	**golule**
cannon	**tup**
disaster	**mosibat**
drought	**khoshk sâli**
earthquake	**zelzele**
famine	**ghaht**
fighter *soldier*	**jangande**
gun: *pistol*	**tapânche**
rifle	**tofang**
cannon	**tup**
machine gun	**mosalsal**
missile	**mushak**
missiles	**mushak-hâ**
mortar	**khompâre**
natural disaster	**mosibat-e tabi'i**
navy	**artesh-e daryâ'i**
nuclear energy	**niru-ye âtomi**
nuclear power station	**nirugâh-e âtomi**
officer	**afsar**
parachute	**parashut**

peace	**solh**
peace-keeping troops	**lashkar-e hâfez-e solh**
people	**mardom**
pistol	**tapânche**
refugee camp	**kâmp-e panâhandegân**
refugee	**panâhande**
refugees	**panâhandegân**
relief aid	**komak-e emdâdi**
rifle	**tofang**
sack	**guni**
shell *of gun*	**khompâre**
submachine gun	**mosalsal-e khodkâr**
tank	**tânk**
troops	**sarbâzân**
unexploded ammunition/	**mohemât-e monfajer**
ordnance	**nashode**
unexploded bomb	**bomb-e monfajer**
	nashode
war	**jang**
weapon	**aslahe**

25. TOOLS

AFZAR

binoculars	**durbin**
brick	**âjor**
brush	**ghalam-e mu**
cable	**kâbl**
charcoal	**zoghâl**
cooker *stove*	**gâz**
hob	**cherâgh**
crowbar	**ahram**
drill	**deril**
hammer	**chakosh**
handle	**dastgir**
hose	**shilang**
insecticide	**hashare-kosh**
ladder	**nardebân**
machine	**mâshin**
microscope	**mikroskop**
nail	**mikh**
padlock	**qofl**
paint	**rang**
pick-ax	**kolang**
plank	**takhte**
plastic	**pelâstik**
pressure cooker	**zud-paz**
rope	**tanâb**
rubber	**lâstik**
rust	**zang**
saw	**are**
scissors	**ghaychi**
screw	**pich**
screwdriver	**pichkoshti**
sewing machine	**mâshin khayâti**

sieve	**âbkesh**
spade	**bil**
spanner/wrench	**âchâr**
straw	**kâh**
string	**nakh**
telescope	**teleskop**
varnish	**vârni; vârnish**
wire	**sim**

Some common expressions . . .

Here are a few expressions you'll hear in everyday conversation:

khob!	well!; okay!
pishkesh!	take it, it's yours!
bâshe!	all right!; okay!
bârikallâh!	bravo!; well done!
ê bâbâ!	oh dear!
(âh) vây!	oh! *in admiration or surprise*
âkh!	ow!
ya'ni...	I mean...; that's to say...
cheghadr hayf shod!	what a pity!
or **hayfe!**	
bas-e!	that's enough!
aslan!	no way!
jedi migi?	you don't say!; really?
cherâ na?	why not?
mas'ale nist!	no problem!
aybi nadâre!	it doesn't matter!
âyâ ... ?	*commonly introduces a question*

26. THE CAR

MASHIN

Where can I rent a car?	**Kojâ mitunam mâshin kerâye konam?**
Where can I rent a car with a driver?	**Kojâ mitunam mâshin bâ rânande kerâye konam?**
How much is it per day?	**Ruzi cheghadr mishe?**
How much is it per week?	**Hafte'i cheghadr mishe?**
Can I park here?	**Mitunam injâ pârk konam?**
Are we on the right road for ... ?	**In râh be taraf-e ... mire?**
Where is the nearest filling station?	**Nazdiktarin pomp-e benzin kojâ-st?**
Fill the tank please.	**Lotfan, por-esh konid.**
normal/diesel	**normâl/dizel**
Check the oil/tires/battery, please.	**Lotfan, rôghan/lâstik/bâtri râ mo'âyene konid.**

—In case of difficulty

I have lost my car keys.	**Man suich-e mâshin râ gom kardom.**
My car has broken down.	**Mâshin-e man kharâb shode.**
There's something wrong with this car.	**In mâshin yek aybi dâre.**
I have a puncture/flat tire.	**Yeki az lâstik-hâ pânchâr shode.**

The tire is flat.	**Lâstik pânchâr e.**
I have run out of petrol/gas.	**Benzinam tamâm shod.**
My car is stuck.	**Mâshin-am gir karde.**
We need a mechanic.	**Ehtiyâj be mekânik dârim.**
Can you tow us?	**Mitavânid mâshin-e-mâ-rô boksol konid?**
Where is the nearest garage?	**Nazdiktarin ta'mirgâh kojâ-st?**
Can you jumpstart the car (by pushing)?	**Mâshin-râ mitunid hôl bedid?**
There's been an accident.	**Tasâdof shode.**
My car has been stolen.	**Mâshin-am-ô dozidand.**
Call the police!	**Polis râ sedâ konid!**
driver's license	**tasdigh-e rânandegi**
insurance policy	**gharârdâd-e bime**
car papers	**madârek-e mâshin**
car registration	**shomâre-ye mâshin**

—Vehicle words

Loghat-ha-ye mashin

accelerator	**gâz**
air	**havâ**
anti-freeze	**zed-e yakh**
axle	**aksal**
battery	**bâtri**
bonnet/hood	**kâput**
boot/trunk	**sandogh-e aghab**
brake	**tormoz**
bumper	**separ**

THE CAR

car park	**pârking**
chains: snow chains	**zanjir-e barf**
clutch	**kalâch**
driver	**rânande**
engine	**motôr**
exhaust	**ekzâst**
fan belt	**tasne-ye parvâne**
gear	**dande**
indicator light	**râhnamâ**
inner tube	**lule-ye dâkheli**
jack	**jâk**
mechanic	**mekânik**
neutral drive	**dande-ye khalâs**
oil	**rôghan**
oilcan	**ghuti-ye rôghan**
passenger	**savâri**
petrol	**benzin**
pump	**pâmp**
radiator	**râdyâtor**
reverse (gear)	**(dande) aghab**
seat	**sandali**
spare tyre/tire	**lâstik-e ezâfe**
speed	**harârat**
steering wheel	**farmân**
tank	**tânk**
tool box	**tôl-baks**
tow rope	**sim-e boksol**
trailer	**terayli**
tyre/tire	**lâstik**
windscreen wipers	**barf pâk-kon**
windscreen/windshield	**shishe**

27. SPORTS

VARZESH

Displays of physical strength are greatly prized in Iranian society. Wrestling (**koshti**), martial arts (**varzesh-e pahlavâni**) and horse-racing are particularly favorite traditional sports, and great tournaments are held, together with great tests of strength — similar to the spirit of the Highland Games in Scotland. More recent sports adopted include skiing, basketball and, of course, soccer.

ball	**tup**
basketball	**bâsketbâl**
chess	**shatranj**
cricket	**kriket**
final	**fâynal**
goal	**gol**
golf	**golf**
horse racing	**mosâbeghe-ye asb;**
	asb davâni
horseback riding	**asb savâri**
match	**mosâbeghe**
soccer match	**mosâbeghe-ye futbol**
pitch	**zamin-e futbol**
referee	**dâvar**
rugby	**râgbi**
skiing	**eski**
soccer/football	**futbol**
stadium	**estâdyum**
swimming	**shenâ**
team	**tim**
Who won?	**Ki bord?**
What's the score?	**Chand-chand hastand?**
Who scored?	**Ki gol zad?**

28. THE BODY

BADAN

ankle	**ghuzak**
arm	**dast**
back	**posht**
beard	**rishe**
blood	**khun**
body	**badan**
bone	**ostokhun**
bottom	**bâsan**
breasts/bust	**pestân**
calf *of leg*	**sâgh-e pâ**
chest	**sine**
cheek	**ru; gune**
chin	**châne**
ear	**gush**
elbow	**ârenj**
eye	**cheshm**
eyebrow	**abru**
eyelashes	**mozhgân**
face	**surat**
finger	**angosht**
fingers	**angosht-hâ**
index finger	**angosht-e neshân**
fist	**mosht**
foot	**pâ**
feet	**pâ-hâ**
genitals	**âlât-e tanâsoli**
hair	**mu**
hand	**dast**
head	**sar**
heart	**ghalb**
jaw	**fak**

kidney	**kolye**
knee	**zânu**
leg	**pâ**
lip	**lab**
liver	**jigar**
lung	**shosh**
mustache	**sebil**
mouth	**dehan**
nail *of finger/toe*	**nâkhon**
navel	**nâf**
neck	**gardan**
nose	**damâgh**
rib	**dande**
shoulder	**shâne**
skin	**pust**
stomach	**shekam**
throat	**gelu**
thumb	**shast**
toe	**angosht-e pâ**
tongue	**zabân**
tooth	**dandân**
teeth	**dandân-hâ**
vein	**rag** *or* **siyâh-rag**
womb	**rahem**
wrist	**moch-e dast**

29. POLITICS

SIYASAT

aid worker	**kârgar-e emdâdi**
ambassador	**safir**
arrest	**dastgir kardan**
assassination	**teror**
assembly *meeting*	**anjoman**
parliament	**majlis**
autonomy	**khod mokhtâri**
ayatollah	**âyatolâh**
cabinet	**kâbine**
charity *organization*	**mo'asese-ye khayriye**
citizen	**tâbe'**
civil rights	**hoghugh-e madani**
civil war	**jang-e dâkheli**
communism	**komunizm**
communist	**komunist**
condemn	**mahkum kardan**
constitution	**mashrutiyat**
convoy	**kârvân**
corruption	**fesâd**
coup d'etat	**kudetâ**
crime	**jorm; jenâyat**
criminal	**jenâyatkâr**
crisis	**bohrân**
dictator	**diktâtôr**
debt	**bedehkâri; qarz**
democracy	**demôkrâsi**
dictatorship	**diktâtôri**
diplomatic ties	**ravâbet-e diplômâtik**
elder (of village etc)	**rish-sefid**
election(s)	**entekhâbât**

embassy	**sefârat**
ethnic cleansing	**koshtar-e nezhâdi**
exile	**tab'id**
free	**âzâd**
freedom	**âzâdi**
government	**hokumat**
guerrilla	**cherik; partizan**
hostage	**gerôgân**
humanitarian aid	**komak-e ensâni**
human rights	**hoghugh-e bashar**
imam	**emâm**
independence	**esteghlâl**
independent	**mostaghel**
independent state	**keshvar-e mostaghel**
judge	**ghâzi**
killer	**âdamkosh; ghâtel**
king	**malek**
law court	**dâdgâh**
law	**ghânun**
lawyer	**vakil**
leader	**rahbar**
left-wing	**chapi**
liberation	**âzâdi**
majority	**aksariyat**
mercenary	**sarbâz-e mozdur**
minister	**vazir**
ministry	**vezârat**
minority	**aghaliyat**
ethnic minority	**aghaliyat-e nezhâdi**
minority vote	**ra'y-e aghaliyat**
murder	**ghatl**
nation	**dôlat; melat**
nationalism	**vatanparasti**
nationalist	**vatanparast**
opposition	**mokhâlefin**

parliament	**majles**
lower house	**majles-e bâlâ**
upper house	**majles-e pâ'in**
Council of Guardians	**Shurâ-ye Negahbân**
(political) party	**hezb (-e siyâsi)**
politics	**siyâsat**
peace	**solh**
peace-keeping troops	**lashkar-e hâfez solh**
politician	**siyâsatmadâr**
president	**ra'is jomhur**
prime minister	**nâkhost vazir**
prison	**zendân**
prisoner-of-war	**asir-e jangi**
prisoner-of-war camp	**ordu-ye asirân-e jangi**
protest *noun*	**mokhâlefat; e'terâz**
Red Crescent	**Helâl-e Ahmar**
Iranian Red Crescent	**Sazemân-e Anjoman-e Helâl-e Ahmar-e Irân**
Red Cross	**Salib-e Sorkh**
refugee	**panâhande**
refugees	**panâhandegân**
revolution	**enghelâb**
right-wing	**jenâh râst**
robbery	**dozdi**
seat *in assembly*	**korsi**
secret police	**polis-e seri**
socialism	**sosyâlizm**
socialist	**sosyâlist**
spy	**jâsus**
state *nation*	**dôlat; melat**
struggle *noun*	**kushesh; ejtehâd**
to testify	**govâhi dâdan; shehâdat dâdan**
theft	**dozdi**

trade union		**etehâdiye-ye asnâf**
treasury		**khazâne**
United Nations		**Sâzemân-e Melal-e Motahed**
veto:	*noun*	**rad**
	verb	**rad kardan**
vote		**ra'y**
vote-rigging		**takhalof-e ra'y**
voting		**ra'y dâdan**

30. TIME & DATES
SA'AT O TARIKH

century	**sade; gharn**
decade	**dôre-ye dah sâleh**
year	**sâl**
month	**mâh**
fortnight	**dô hafte**
week	**hafte**
day	**ruz**
hour	**sâ'at**
minute	**daghighe**
second	**sâniye**
dawn	**fajr**
sunrise	**tolu'**
morning	**sobh**
daytime	**ruz**
noon	**zohr**
afternoon	**ba'd az zohr**
evening	**asr; ghorub**
sunset	**ghorub-e âftâb**
night	**shab**
midnight	**nim-e shab**
three days before	**seh ruz pish**
the day before yesterday	**pariruz**
yesterday	**diruz**
today	**emruz**
tomorrow	**fardâ**
the day after tomorrow	**pasfardâ**
three days from now	**se ruz dige**

TIME & DATES

the year before last	**piyârsâl**
last year	**pârsâl**
this year	**emsâl**
next year	**sâl-e âyande**
the year after next	**dô sâl dige**
last week	**hafte-ye gozashte**
this week	**in hafte**
next week	**hafte-ye dige**
last night	**dishab**
this morning	**emruz sobh**
now	**al'ân; hâlâ**
just now	**hamin al'ân**
this afternoon	**emruz ba'd az zohr**
this evening	**emruz asri**
tonight	**emshab**
yesterday morning	**diruz sobh**
yesterday afternoon	**diruz ba'd az zohr**
yesterday night	**dishab**
tomorrow morning	**fardâ sobh**
tomorrow afternoon	**fardâ ba'd az zohr**
tomorrow night	**fardâ shab**
in the morning	**sobh**
in the afternoon	**ba'd az zohr**
in the evening	**asr**
past	**gozashte**
present	**hâl-e hâzer;**
	zamân-e hâzer
future	**âyande**
What day is it?	**Che ruzi ye?**
What date is it today?	**Emruz chandom e?**
What time is it?	**Sâ'at chand e?**
It is ... o'clock.	**Sâ'at ... e.**

TIME & DATES

—Days of the week
Ruz-ha-ye hafte

Monday	**Dôshambe**
Tuesday	**Sehshambe**
Wednesday	**Chahârshambe**
Thursday	**Panjshambe**
Friday	**Jom'e**
Saturday	**Shambe**
Sunday	**Yekshambe**

—Months
Mah-ha

January	**Zhânviye**
February	**Fevriye**
March	**Mârs**
April	**Âvril**
May	**Mey**
June	**Zhu'an**
July	**Zhu'iye**
August	**'Ut**
September	**Septambr**
October	**Oktôbr**
November	**Novambr**
December	**Desambr**

—Iranian months
Mah-ha-ye Irani

The names of the (solar) months used in Iran correspond to the signs of the zodiac. The Iranian year starts on March 21 — **Nô Ruz** or New Year.

Farvardin
Ordibehesht
Khordad
Tir
Mordâd

Shahrivar
Mehr
Âbân
Âzar
Day
Bahman
Esfand

—Islamic months

Mah-ha-ye Eslami

Dates are also reckoned according to the Islamic calendar, which comprises 12 lunar months. **Ramazân** ("Ramadan") is the month when Muslims fast, **Zulhaj** is the month when Muslims traditionally go on the hajj — the pilgrimage to Mecca.

Muharam *(the first month)*
Safar
Rabi' ul-Aval
Rabi' ul-Âkher
Jamâdi ul-Aval
Jamâdi ul-Âkher
Rajab
Sha'abân
Ramazân
Shavâl
Zulghida
Zulhaj *(the last month)*

31. NUMBERS

SHOMARE-HA

0	**sefr**
1	**yek**
2	**dô**
3	**seh**
4	**chahâr** (*or, conversationally,* **châr**)
5	**panj**
6	**shesh**
7	**haft**
8	**hasht**
9	**noh**
10	**dah**
11	**yâzdah**
12	**davâzdah**
13	**sizdah**
14	**chahârdah**
15	**pânzdah**
16	**shânzdah**
17	**hivdah**
18	**hijdah**
19	**nuzdah**
20	**bist**
21	**bist-o yek**
22	**bist-o dô**
23	**bist-o seh**
24	**bist-o chahâr**
25	**bist-o panj**
26	**bist-o shesh**
27	**bist-o haft**
28	**bist-o hasht**

29	**bist-o noh**
30	**si**
31	**si-o yek**
32	**si-o dô**
33	**si-o seh**
34	**si-o chahâr**
35	**si-o panj**
36	**si-o shesh**
37	**si-o haft**
38	**si-o hasht**
39	**si-o noh**
40	**chehel**
41	**chehel-o yek**
42	**chehel-o dô**
43	**chehel-o seh**
44	**chehel-o chahâr**
45	**chehel-o panj**
46	**chehel-o shesh**
47	**chehel-o haft**
48	**chehel-o hasht**
49	**chehel-o noh**
50	**panjâh**
51	**panjâh-o yek**
52	**panjâh-o dô**
53	**panjâh-o seh**
54	**panjâh-o chahâr**
55	**panjâh-o panj**
56	**panjâh-o shesh**
57	**panjâh-o haft**
58	**panjâh-o hasht**
59	**panjâh-o noh**
60	**shast**

61	shasht-o yek
62	shasht-o dô
63	shasht-o seh
64	shasht-o chahâr
65	shasht-o panj
66	shasht-o shesh
67	shasht-o haft
68	shasht-o hasht
69	shasht-o noh
70	haftâd
71	haftâd-o yek
72	haftâd-o dô
73	haftâd-o seh
74	haftâd-o chahâr
75	haftâd-o panj
76	haftâd-o shesh
77	haftâd-o haft
78	haftâd-o hasht
79	haftâd-o noh
80	hashtâd
81	hashtâd-o yek
82	hashtâd-o dô
83	hashtâd-o seh
84	hashtâd-o chahâr
85	hashtâd-o panj
86	hashtâd-o shesh
87	hashtâd-o haft
88	hashtâd-o hasht
89	hashtâd-o noh
90	navad
91	navad-o yek
92	navad-o dô

93	**navad-o seh**
94	**navad-o chahâr**
95	**navad-o panj**
96	**navad-o shesh**
97	**navad-o haft**
98	**navad-o hasht**
99	**navad-o noh**
100	**sad**
102	**sad-o dô**
112	**sad-o davâz-dah**
200	**davist**
300	**sisad**
400	**chahârsad**
500	**pânsad**
600	**sheshsad**
700	**haftsad**
800	**hashtsad**
900	**nohsad**
1,000	**hezâr**
2,000	**dô hezâr**
3,000	**seh hezâr**
4,000	**chahâr hezâr**
5,000	**panj hezâr**
6,000	**shesh hezâr**
7,000	**haft hezâr**
8,000	**hasht hezâr**
9,000	**noh hezâr**
10,000	**dah hezâr**
50,000	**panjâh hezâr**
100,000	**sad hezâr**
1,000,000	**milyôn**

first	**aval**
second	**dôvom**
third	**sevom**
fourth	**chahârom**
fifth	**panjom**
sixth	**sheshom**
seventh	**haftom**
eighth	**hashtom**
ninth	**nôhom**
tenth	**dahom**
twentieth	**bistom**
once	**yekbâr**
twice	**dôbâr**
three times	**sehbâr**
one-half	**nesf**
one-third	**yek sevom**
two-thirds	**dô sevom**
one-quarter	**rob'**
three-quarters	**seh rob'**

32. OPPOSITES
ANTONIM-HA

beginning—end	**shoru'—âkhar**
clean—dirty	**tamiz—kasif**
comfortable—uncomfortable	**râhat—nârâhat**
fertile—barren *land*	**hâselkhiz—bihâsel** *or* **khoshk**
happy—unhappy	**khosh-hâl—nârâhat**
life—death	**zendegi—marg**
friend—enemy	**dust—doshman**
modern—traditional	**modern—sonati**
modern—ancient	**modern—ghadimi**
open—shut	**bâz—baste**
wide—narrow	**pahn—bârik**
high—low	**boland—pâ'in/kutâh**
peace—violence/war	**solh—khoshunat/jang**
polite—rude	**mo'adab—bitarbiyat**
silence—noise	**sokut—sedâ**
cheap—expensive	**arzân—gerân**
hot/warm—cold/cool	**garm—sard**
health—disease	**salâmat—marizi**
well—sick	**sâlem—mariz**
night—day	**shab—ruz**
top—bottom	**bâlâ—tâh**
backwards—forwards	**aghab—jelô**
back—front	**posht—ru**
dead—alive	**morde—zende**
near—far	**nazdik—dur**
left—right	**chap—râst**
inside—outside	**tu—birun**

up—down	**bâlâ—pâ'in**
yes—no	**bale—nah/nakhayr**
here—there	**injâ—ânjâ**
soft—hard	**narm—seft**
easy—difficult	**âsân—sakht**
quick—slow	**sari'/tond—yavâsh**
big—small	**bozorg—kuchek**
old—young	**pir—javân**
tall—short *people*	**ghad boland—**
	ghad kutâh
tall—short *things*	**boland—kutâh**
strong—weak	**ghavi—za'if**
success—failure	**movafaghiyat—nâkâmi**
new—old	**nô—kohne**
question—answer	**so'âl—javâb**
safety—danger	**amniyat—khatar**
good—bad	**khob—bad**
true—false	**dorost—nâdorost**
light—heavy	**sabok—sangin**
light—darkness	**nur—târiki**
well—badly	**khob—kharâb**
truth—lie	**haghighat—dorugh**

Tajik-English/English-Tajik
Practical Dictionary
ISBN 978-0-7818-1233-X · $22.95pb

Turkmen-English/English-Turkmen
Dictionary & Phrasebook
4,000 entries · ISBN 978-0-7818-1072-2 · $11.95pb

Urdu-English/English-Urdu
Dictionary & Phrasebook (*Romanized*)
3,000 entries · ISBN 0-7818-0970-3 · $14.95pb

Uzbek-English/English-Uzbek
Dictionary & Phrasebook
3,000 entries · ISBN 978- 0-7818-0959-X ·
$13.95pb

Uzbek-English/English-Uzbek
Concise Dictionary
7,500 entries · ISBN 0-7818-0165-6 · $15.95pb

Uzbek-English/English-Uzbek
Practical Dictionary
20,000 entries · ISBN 0-7818-1325-5 · $29.95pb

Arabic-English/English-Arabic
Dictionary & Phrasebook
4,500 entries · ISBN 0-7818-0973-8 · $14.95pb

Arabic-English/English-Arabic
Practical Dictionary
18,000 entries · ISBN 0-7818-1045-0 · $27.50pb

Mastering Arabic 1 with 2 Audio CDs:
3rd Edition
ISBN 0-7818-1338-7 · $40.00pb

Mastering Arabic 2 with 2 Audio CDs:
An Intermediate Course
ISBN: 978-0-7818-1254-2 · $32.00pb

Mastering Arabic 1 Activity Book
ISBN 978-0-7818-1339-6 · $19.95pb

Beginner's Iraqi Arabic with 2 Audio CDs
ISBN 0-7818-1098-1 · $29.95pb

English-Arabic/Arabic-English
Modern Military Dictionary
11,000 entries · ISBN 0-7818-0243-1 · $16.95p

Pocket Guide to Arabic Script
ISBN 0-7818-1104-X · $9.95pb